a passion for
ICE CREAM

Emily Luchetti

a passion for
ICE CREAM

95 RECIPES *for* FABULOUS DESSERTS

WITHDRAWN

EMILY LUCHETTI

photographs *by* **SHERI GIBLIN**

CHRONICLE BOOKS
SAN FRANCISCO

Library of Congress Cataloging-in-Publication
Data available.

ISBN 0-8118-4602-4

Manufactured in China.

Designed by Brooke Johnson
Prop styling by Leigh Noe
Food styling by Dan Becker
Food styling assistance by Kate Christ
Photography assistance by Selena Aument
Typeset in FF Profile and Bell

"Dream Ice Cream Machine"
courtesy of Sur La Table.

PHOTOGRAPHER'S ACKNOWLEDGMENTS
I'd first like to thank Emily Luchetti, who not only
worked alongside us in the studio day after day,
but made sure we tasted each and every one of those
fabulous ice cream desserts. I'd also like to thank
Chronicle Books and my awesome team of stylists
and assistants—without them none of these
photos would be possible.

Distributed in Canada by Raincoast Books
9050 Shaughnessy Street
Vancouver, British Columbia V6P 6E5

10 9 8 7 6 5 4 3 2 1

Chronicle Books LLC
85 Second Street
San Francisco, California 94105

www.chroniclebooks.com

to Mark,
whose vision and passion
for food, both savory and
sweet, is an inspiration.

CONTENTS

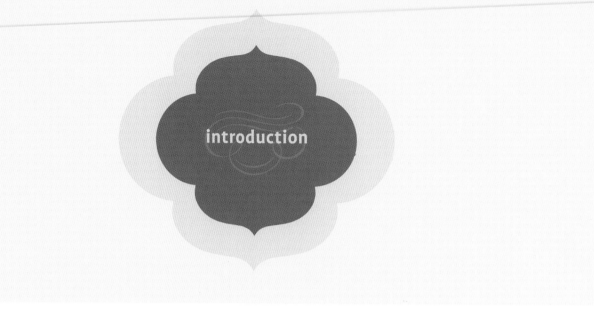

introduction

Imagine the dreariness of a world without ice cream. There would be nothing floating in a root beer float, no à la mode, nothing cold and sweet waiting in the freezer on sleepless nights, no melted remnants to suck out of the bottom of sugar cones, no more nut and cherry garnishes topping a mound of whipped cream.

Fortunately, we don't have to worry about this scary scenario, as ice cream is firmly embedded in our culture. In fact, our infatuation with ice cream and all its related categories (sorbets, sherbet, frozen yogurt, and other frozen sweets) has for all practical purposes created its own food group. Each person in this country on average consumes forty-six pints annually. All of us—extrovert or introvert, toddler or grandparent—crave frozen desserts for the same reason. Why? They taste fantastic.

As a professional pastry chef, I, too, am passionate about frozen treats. Whether I am creating new recipes at Farallon restaurant or baking desserts at home, I can press my lips together and say no to fresh fruit tarts, warm chocolate cakes, and even buttery shortbread. But put any freshly churned ice cream or sorbet in front of me, and my fingers itch for a spoon. In a desperate attempt to leave room for something else in my diet (and leave a little ice cream for the diners in the restaurant), I spin (pastry chef slang for *churn*) the ice cream in the early morning before my sweet taste buds wake up. Like everyone else, I have to limit my bites, so I try to make each bite the best I've ever tasted. There's no place for wimpy flavors or airy texture.

That's where *homemade* ice cream comes in. What makes it better than store bought is its intense fresh taste and creamy texture, without stabilizers.

Although most people prefer homemade ice cream, many have never made it. This is surprising, because you don't need to be a pastry chef to make ice cream. With the right recipe, it's pretty simple. With affordable electric machines available, you don't even have to hand crank homemade ice cream anymore (unless you are an old-fashioned purist). Some frozen desserts, such as granitas, semifreddos, frozen pops, and parfaits, can be made without an ice cream machine.

The advantages of making your own are many. When you make homemade ice cream, you, not the manufacturer, can decide how much of your favorite chocolate chunks to add. You can take advantage of the succulent sweet peaches you found at the farmers' market or adjust spices as your palate prefers. In sorbets and granitas, fresh seasonal fruit puréed and frozen at home bursts with flavor beyond anything a food scientist could create. And, ice cream tastes best licked straight off the dasher or after it's been in the freezer for a couple of hours, when it's scoopable but not rock hard. With store-bought, you don't get it in its perfect state.

It's creative, too. After making ice cream a couple of times, you will learn the basics and can invent flavors of your own. More than any other kind of dessert preparation, ice cream making allows the most experimentation with the most delicious results.

Although ice cream's popularity is undisputed, a simple discussion about preferences can end in a brawl, as fans of mint chocolate chip, butter pecan, cookie dough, and vanilla try to convert the less enlightened. To include as many flavors as possible, I have not used the same one twice in a recipe, except in the case of vanilla, which complements more-dominant flavors and is a building block for many desserts. I offer two vanilla recipes, French Vanilla and Rich Vanilla. Make both and see which you like better.

Sometimes, you crave just a simple bowl of ice cream or sorbet. Nothing fancy—just a couple of scoops to savor as you settle into your favorite chair to read a novel or watch a movie. With this in mind, I have listed all the ice cream and sorbet flavors in the book and their page numbers in a chart on page 215. Select a flavor and make just the ice cream or sorbet part of the recipe.

You can serve ice cream in hundreds of ways: in a sandwich or on a stick, in a shake or with a cake, or as part of a plated dessert. Layer ginger cookies and lemon ice cream, top pineapple granita with ginger beer sabayon, drop scoops of white chocolate ice cream into iced espresso, or serve chocolate crepes with peppermint ice cream, and you have only begun to explore the possibilities for ice cream desserts.

Of course, ice cream must be made in advance. While this does require some planning, it works to your benefit as the ice cream can be made around your schedule. Make the ice cream base when you have some time, freeze it the next day, and by dinner you will be scooping it out for your appreciative guests.

Another compelling reason to make homemade ice cream is to re-create the taste and spirit of independent ice cream shops across the country. They make ice cream with high-quality ingredients and take great pride in their selections, just as we do when making ice cream at home. We have all piled into the car on a muggy summer evening to go to our local ice cream stand for that ultimate pick-me-up. It is about the delicious ice cream as well as the social camaraderie. Throughout the book, I have profiled seven of my favorite artisanal ice cream shops. This is not an exhaustive list, as there are many fabulous ice cream shops in the United States.

One of my earliest ice cream memories was listening intently for the tinkle of the bell on the Good Humor truck at dusk on a summer evening. As I saw it turn onto the block, I ran for the corner, pushing aside my siblings and cousins, determined to be the first to be there when Ray, the driver, stopped. My grandfather patiently followed behind the fray, reaching for his wallet. I anxiously read the offerings, and after much internal debate made my selection of a chocolate éclair bar. In that moment, life was just about ice cream and the pleasure it brings. Thirty-five years later, I still feel that way when anticipating and eating ice cream. I hope these recipes help bring back your own recollections of ice cream and help you create many more. The purpose of this book is to promote good ice cream in and out of the home. Pass your favorite recipes on to your friends and even strangers. They will be happy you did.

frozen dessert
descriptions

The federal government has established minimum standards for commercial ice cream production. It is beneficial to understand these, as they help identify how to make homemade ice cream taste its absolute best.

Without cream, you can't have **ice cream**. By law, ice cream must have at least 10 percent milk fat, but ice cream made with the minimum fat really isn't worth eating. Ice cream needs more fat to taste like ice cream should taste: cool and smooth. Most of the fat in ice cream comes from cream, and it provides not only flavor but also texture. However, there is a point where ice cream can have *too* much fat, making it too rich and heavy, and that's why milk is also added.

When ice cream is churned, air is mixed into it. The amount of air added is called *overrun*. In home machines, little air is incorporated. Less air makes denser ice cream. Many commercial ice cream manufacturers pump air into their ice cream during production. Cheaper ice cream, both in price and quality, has high overrun. Ice cream, by law, must weigh at least 4 ½ pounds per gallon, not including any mix-ins, and its volume can increase by 100 percent. That's half ice cream, half air. Who wants to eat or pay for air? Pick up a gallon of high-overrun ice cream, and you quickly notice how light it is compared to homemade. One scoop of homemade ice cream offers more pleasure than a full bowl of high-overrun ice cream.

Since homemade ice cream is consumed relatively quickly, stabilizers are not needed. Stabilizers are used in commercial ice creams, sorbets, and sherbets to help them remain smooth. They aren't necessarily a bad thing; it just depends on what kind and how much are used. By law, stabilizers cannot make up more than 5 percent of an ice cream's weight. As the amount of fat decreases, more stabilizers are added to keep the ice cream creamy. Natural stabilizers are better than those made from chemicals. You will be able to tell if a frozen dessert has too many stabilizers. It will taste artificial, and the texture will be gummy and stretchy.

The quality of commercial frozen ice creams, sherbets, and sorbets varies widely. Read labels and compare different brands. Premium ice cream has more fat and less overrun than regular ice cream. Super-premium products are closer to homemade than those made to minimum standards.

There are two types of ice cream: Philadelphia style, which is made without eggs, and French (or custard), which has a custard base of egg yolks cooked with milk and cream. Both are equally good; they are just different. It is a personal matter which you prefer. I have included both types in this book, and all the flavors can be made either way.

Sorbets consist of sugar, water, and flavoring ingredients, most often fruit purées. They don't have fat unless a particular ingredient, such as coconut or chocolate, is used.

Granita has the same ingredients as sorbet, but it is frozen in a pan in the freezer (called *still freezing*). As the mixture freezes, it is periodically mixed with a fork to break up the ice crystals. This gives granitas a feathery-light texture. Unlike sorbets, they are not smooth, but icy. They are cool and refreshing.

Sherbet is made with dairy products, but has less fat than ice cream. It is primarily made in fruit flavors.

Frozen yogurt, which is usually mixed with other dairy ingredients to yield a smooth texture, is very popular as a soft-serve product in ice cream and frozen yogurt shops.

In France, **parfaits** are frozen desserts made of several flavors of cooked custards that are layered in tall glasses. In the United States, they are more like sundaes, with layered ice cream, sauces, and fruit.

Semifreddos are Italian in origin; the word translates as "half frozen." Semifreddos are still-frozen.

Frozen custard is especially popular in the Midwest. Like French ice cream, it must have a fat content of at least 10 percent and contain 1.4 percent egg yolks. The egg yolks make it smooth and creamy. It's served soft-serve style, but has less air, a more velvety texture, and a cleaner taste than commercial soft-serve ice cream. Soft-serve is served slightly warmer than ice cream. It is made daily and is generally not carried over to the next day.

Low-fat, light, and **reduced-fat ice creams** are just what they imply, ice cream with less fat. Since fat is crucial to good ice cream, my opinion of low-fat ice cream is why bother? Lower-fat ice cream just reminds me of what I am missing and still has quite a bit of fat. If I am watching my calories, I will have sherbet, sorbet, or granita and save ice cream for a later splurge.

Italian **gelato** is one of the sweet wonders of the world. It has less fat, less air, less sugar, and more intense flavor than ice cream. It is not served as cold as ice cream. Produced in small batches, it uses the finest ingredients and is an artisanal product, like ice cream made at home. *Gelato* is a generic term that includes both cream- and noncream-based frozen desserts. In Italy, there isn't just one type of gelato, there are several, which vary from region to region. In the United States, the term *gelato* is used loosely. Italian bakeries and scoop shops adhere more strictly to the Italian specifications. The ice cream in this book is more like gelato than commercial ice cream, but it is not true gelato. I leave gelato making to the Italians and concentrate on making the best-tasting American ice cream I can.

getting started:
*ingredients, ice cream
machines, and other
equipment*

ingredients

When going to the store to buy ingredients for frozen desserts, you can use the express line for checkout, as they don't require many ingredients. But, as in all desserts, quality is important for great-tasting results.

Berries: Use fragrant, juicy berries for sorbets and ice creams. Search for local, organic fruit. Its aroma and flavor are superior. Off season, you can use frozen raspberries and blackberries in sauces, sorbets, and ice creams. Be sure to buy frozen berries without added sugar or syrup. Frozen strawberries don't have the same flavor as frozen blackberries and raspberries.

Butter: I always use unsalted butter in baking, because it allows me to regulate the amount of salt. High-fat butters, while delicious in pastries, are not used in ice cream making. There's enough fat in the cream.

Chocolate: I use bittersweet chocolate and prefer it over semisweet. Generally, the latter is too sweet, and this extra sweetness dulls the flavor. The one exception is the semisweet chocolate made by Scharffen Berger. It is wonderful and has changed the way I look at semisweet. Chocolate brands I recommend are Callebaut, Dagoba Organic, El Rey, E. Guittard, Scharffen Berger, and Vahlrona. If you can find good-quality chocolate in chunks or chips, purchase it—otherwise, chop your own. I like Guittard's double-chocolate chips.

Citrus juices: Always use freshly squeezed lemon, lime, and orange juices. The flavors are much brighter and do not have a negative aftertaste like artificially flavored juices or those made from concentrate.

Cocoa powder: My favorite is Vahlrona, but it can be hard to find in retail shops. Droste and Ghirardelli also make good unsweetened cocoa powder.

Coconut: Sweetened coconut is too sweet to use in desserts. Using unsweetened coconut controls the amount of sugar and produces desserts with a stronger coconut taste and a crisper texture. Look for it in natural foods stores. Coconut milk is unsweetened and is used in Thai cooking. Coconut cream is sweetened and thicker than coconut milk and is used frequently in alcoholic drinks.

toasting coconut: Place the coconut in a single layer on a parchment paper–lined baking sheet. Bake in a preheated 350°F oven for 5 minutes, then stir the coconut and continue to bake another 2 to 3 minutes, or until evenly golden brown. Watch the coconut carefully, as it burns quickly, especially around the edges.

Coffee: I use coffee in different forms, depending on the recipe. I infuse cracked whole coffee beans for a deep flavor, add ground coffee for a short infusion, use instant espresso (preferably Medaglia d'Oro) when I need it as a dry ingredient, and use room-temperature brewed coffee when I require a liquid in a recipe. If you are using large instant coffee crystals, crush them slightly before adding to help them dissolve quicker. I always use decaffeinated coffees.

Cream: Not surprisingly, cream is the most important ingredient in ice cream making. Use heavy (whipping) cream. Avoid ultrapasteurized whenever possible, even if you have to go out of your way to do so. Some chain supermarkets sell only ultrapasteurized, but regular heavy cream can be found at many grocery stores including Whole Foods, Trader Joe's, and specialty grocery stores. If your store does not carry it, request it. If enough people inquire, they will stock it. Organic cream makes especially delicious ice cream.

Crème fraîche: Crème fraîche, a cultured cream, is becoming more readily available in grocery stores. It has a great tangy flavor that complements ice cream well and cuts the fatty taste in many desserts and ice creams. If you don't see crème fraîche in your grocery store, ask for it and convince them to buy it. It can be used in savory cooking as well. If you want to make your own, for each cup of cream, stir in

1 tablespoon of buttermilk. Cover and let sit on the counter for 24 hours. Stir and let sit another 24 hours. At this point, it should be thick. Refrigerate until ready to use.

Dulce de leche and **cajeta:** Dulce de leche originates from Argentina and is made from cow's milk. Cajeta is from Mexico and is made with goat's milk. Both are made by slowly cooking milk for hours until the natural sugars in the milk caramelize. Cajeta and dulce de leche are interchangeable in the recipes in this book (see Sources). You can make your own dulce de leche from sweet condensed milk. Many recipes are available online.

Eggs: Large eggs were used in all the recipes in this book. If you use other sizes of eggs, go by weight, not quantity. A large egg yolk weighs about ¾ of an ounce, a large white about 1 ½ ounces. If desired, pasteurized egg whites are available for recipes that use uncooked egg whites (see Sources).

Filo: The flakiness of filo is a nice contrast to ice cream and sorbets. Some large cities still have bakeries that sell fresh filo. If you can find fresh, by all means buy it. Store-bought filo can be found in the frozen section of your grocery store. Defrost filo overnight in the refrigerator. Filo sheets come in different sizes, depending on how it is cut and packaged by the manufacturer.

Half-and-half: Many ice cream recipes call for half-and-half. Instead of buying one more product at the store, I use half milk and half cream in any recipe that requires it.

Mascarpone: Made both in Italy and the United States, this creamy cheese is worth every calorie. Use carefully in ice cream, as its high fat content can make ice cream too fatty and cause it to separate.

Milk: Save 2 percent or skim milk for cereal. Whole milk is needed in ice cream for the creaminess. Anything less than whole milk will make a thin, icy ice cream.

Nuts: Nuts are interchangeable in recipes, so use the ones you like best. Always toast nuts before using. This brings out their flavor and keeps them from getting soggy when used in desserts.

toasting nuts: Place them in a single layer on a baking sheet. Bake in a pre-heated 350°F oven for about 10 minutes, or until fragrant and lightly browned. Nuts with a higher fat content toast more quickly.

skinning hazelnuts and pistachios: To remove the skin from toasted hazelnuts and pistachios, rub them in a colander. The slight ridges on the holes easily clean the nuts, and the flaky skin falls through the holes.

Passion fruit: In season, you can use fresh passion fruit. You can also use unsweetened purée. To purée fresh passion fruit, cut the passion fruit in half and scoop out the insides. Purée in a food processor and then strain. The little black seeds are edible, but I don't use them in ice cream. (See Sources for purée and fresh passion fruit.)

Peanuts, Spanish: These small red-skinned peanuts are traditionally used in tin roof sundaes. They are the perfect size for desserts, and the skin comes off easily. Skin them like hazelnuts, above.

Pomegranate juice: POMWonderful makes pomegranate juice and distributes it throughout the United States.

Rose water: The best rose water is Persian, from Kashan, with the finest aroma and concentration. Other good-quality rose waters are Cortas, which uses Lebanese roses, and one made by Sadef Company in California.

Salt: I prefer kosher salt for baking (and cooking). It heightens flavors without an iodine or strong salty taste. It also dissolves quickly. The granules are too big to fit through a sifter when sifting dry ingredients, so add it after sifting.

Seltzer water: I use seltzer water in my soda recipes because it has a clean effervescence. This neutral background allows the primary flavors to shine. You can buy seltzer or purchase a Thermos-type container with CO_2 chargers and make your own (see Sources, page 216). Club soda does not have the same clean flavor. Seltzer water is available in most grocery stores.

Soy milk: Soy milk is very good for you. Using it in frozen desserts is a great way for lactose-intolerant individuals to enjoy frozen desserts. I use plain, not flavored, soy milk in the recipes.

Spices: I like to use both whole and ground spices. I infuse cinnamon sticks and cardamom pods in liquid for a rich flavor, and add them in ground form for extra punch. Using only ground spice doesn't make for a deeply flavored ice cream. Make sure to use your spices regularly. Those dug out of the back of your cabinet won't have as much flavor as recently purchased spices.

Sugar, granulated: Pure cane sugar is the best; always make sure to use it. You can use baker's or superfine sugar, but it isn't necessary. Cane sugar is essential for nicely textured ice cream, as it helps keep ice cream smooth. Artificial sweeteners make hard ice cream and should be avoided.

Sugar, brown: I prefer dark brown sugar for maximum brown sugar flavor.

Tapioca pearls: Large tapioca pearls are used in bubble tea. Find them in Asian grocery stores or see Sources, page 216.

Vanilla: Vanilla beans are expensive. That being said, however, there is nothing like the real thing. It is better to go without than to use imitation vanilla. In vanilla ice cream, especially, it is crucial to use good vanilla beans and extract, for this is where the flavor comes from. To store vanilla beans, put them in a resealable plastic bag, seal, and then put into a second bag and seal.

Wines: Dessert wines, liqueurs, and rum are delicious in and served with ice cream. Use these recipes as guidelines and create your own flavors if you have a little left in a bottle or as an excuse to try something new. Use liqueurs and alcohol sparingly, as their flavors are strong.

Yogurt: Make sure to use unsweetened plain yogurt, either full fat or low fat, whichever you prefer. I like whole fat, as it has a better consistency when frozen.

equipment

Ice cream making requires relatively little equipment beyond an ice cream machine. What you serve the ice cream with may call for more, but as with all baking the equipment is flexible and interchangeable.

ICE CREAM MACHINES

If I received frequent flyer miles for all the batches of ice cream I have churned over the years, I would surely be eligible for a free ticket around the world. On this stationary voyage, I have used many kinds of ice cream machines. The good news is that there isn't just one machine that makes good ice cream. If you don't use an ice cream machine and just pour the base into a pan and freeze it, you will get a very icy ice cream. The constant turning of the ice cream base in an ice cream machine as it freezes breaks up the ice crystals that form and makes the ice cream smooth.

Machine options depend on your budget and how technologically involved you want to get. Most machines use one of three different methods: they freeze the ice cream using rock salt and ice, or a prefrozen insert, or a built-in freezing unit. Once you understand the different kinds, you can choose which works best for your lifestyle (see Sources). Whatever style you get, make sure it has at least a 1½-quart capacity. The recipes in this book were written for this size. If you have a smaller machine, reserve some of the base and churn a second batch. You can increase the recipes for a larger machine.

Machines Using Ice and Rock Salt

White Mountain is the best of this type of machine. It makes some of the best-textured ice cream possible. Available in 4- and 6-quart models, either hand crank or electric, it produces ice cream for a large number of people. I use one whenever I want a big batch of ice cream. It's my party ice cream machine. But you can also make small batches. The metal container is put into the bucket, the base is poured in, the motor is latched on top, and ice and rock salt are layered in the bucket around the canister. Rock salt dissolves slowly, and its coarse consistency keeps it from settling to the bottom of the bucket. Use 1 part rock salt to 8 parts ice. Some people feel it is a bit of a hassle to layer the rock salt and ice, but this is outweighed by the superiority of the ice cream. The machine can also be a bit noisy. I use it on my back porch to keep the dripping ice and the noise to a minimum. I look at the whirring of the motor as a pleasant reminder that there will soon be homemade ice cream to enjoy. After you have used it several times, you will be able to let the sound of the motor tell you when the ice cream is finished. Be sure to rinse out the wooden barrel after use to eliminate salt corrosion.

Many people believe this kind of machine is the only way to make ice cream. Some even scoff at the idea of using an electric version, preferring the hand-cranked model. Ice cream made in this type of machine requires less time hardening in the freezer before serving.

Machines Using Freezer Inserts

The KitchenAid and Cuisinart machines both use prefrozen inserts. Relatively inexpensive, they make good ice cream, are less noisy, and don't take up much room in your kitchen. The KitchenAid model is an attachment to the KitchenAid stand mixer. The Cuisinart model consists of the insert and a base motor. If you have the Cuisinart machine, it's a smart idea to get an additional insert so that you can make two batches of ice cream one right after the other. The down side of these machines is that the inserts stay frozen only long enough to make a 1½-quart batch. Inserts need to be frozen for 8 to 12 hours before using. They must be frozen solid; if you hear any liquid sloshing in the inner layer, they are not ready. Keep the inserts in the freezer at all times so you will be ready to make ice cream whenever you like. It's frustrating to go into your kitchen ready to make ice cream only to discover that you forgot to pre-freeze the unit. The inserts are easy to clean and just need to be hand washed.

Machines Using Built-in Freon Units

The BMWs of ice cream makers have a Freon unit built into the machine. They can make ice cream all day without stopping. No ice and rock salt or prefreezing is neces-sary. Pour the ingredients into the machine, turn it on, and within 20 minutes you will have freshly churned ice cream and be ready to make the next batch. For true ice cream aficionados, this is *the* type of machine to have. I especially like the Lello and Lussino brands. Made of stainless steel, they are sleek, beautiful machines. Freon-based machines take up quite a bit of counter space and are more expensive than the other two types of machines, but if you want to make homemade ice cream with minimal fuss at a moment's notice, this is the kind to buy.

OTHER EQUIPMENT FOR FROZEN DESSERT MAKING

Blenders: Traditionally used for making milk shakes. You can use a food processor, but blenders give you a finer texture. In the case of Batido de Trigo (page 97), a blender is needed for the proper consistency.

Blowtorch: Professional pastry chefs use construction-sized propane torches. They work well but can be a bit awkward for the home cook. Fortunately, small butane torches designed for home kitchen use are available. Propane torches can be found at hardware stores and butane torches at cookware shops.

Bowls: I use stainless-steel bowls for mixing. They are unbreakable, easy to care for, do not pick up odors, and their wide shape makes mixing easy. They can handle either hot or cold ingredients.

Food processor: Good for puréeing fruit and grinding nuts. I prefer making dough by hand or in a stand mixer. The food processor can overwork dough very quickly, so if you do use one, pay close attention and do not overprocess.

Freezers: Unless you eat all the ice cream you make right out of the machine, you will need a freezer. There are numerous brands available; whichever kind you have, make sure your freezer is cold enough. It should be at 0°F. My father-in-law, a butcher who sold freezers with sides of beef in the 1950s and 1960s, never used a thermometer in his freezers. He would buy a quart of ice cream, and if it stayed in good condition, he knew his freezer was cold enough. If it isn't cold enough, ice crystals will form, making the ice cream icy.

Ice cream scoops: Get as many sizes as you can find. You will find a use for all of them. They are fun and functional. I like to use those with a release latch. Zyliss and KitchenAid make great scoops.

Ice cream spades: These are good for scraping ice cream out of a container and also for when you want to serve a wedge, rather than a round scoop. Select a heavy spade so it, not you, does the work of getting the ice cream out of the container.

Microplane: Use to zest citrus and grate nutmeg. They are much easier to use than a regular grater and make finer particles than a zester.

Ovens: While I prefer electric convection ovens, regular gas and electric ovens also work well. It is a good idea to put an oven thermometer in your oven so you can see that the actual temperature matches the temperature you set it at. If it does not, have it calibrated by an oven repair person. If you don't have a convection oven and are baking two baking sheets at a time, it will be necessary to rotate the items halfway through for even baking. If you are using one baking sheet, place it in the center of the oven. With some convection ovens, it is necessary to lower the temperature by 25°F from what is stated in the recipe. When you get a new oven, you can also bake one of your trusted recipes at 350°F, see how it performs, and adjust the temperature accordingly.

Pans: Basic pans include a 9-inch springform pan, a 6-cup loaf pan, a 9-inch square pan, and a 9-by-13-inch pan. I like large (about 3½ inches wide) muffin cups for individual cakes. I like rimmed baking sheets with 1-inch sides (also called jelly-roll

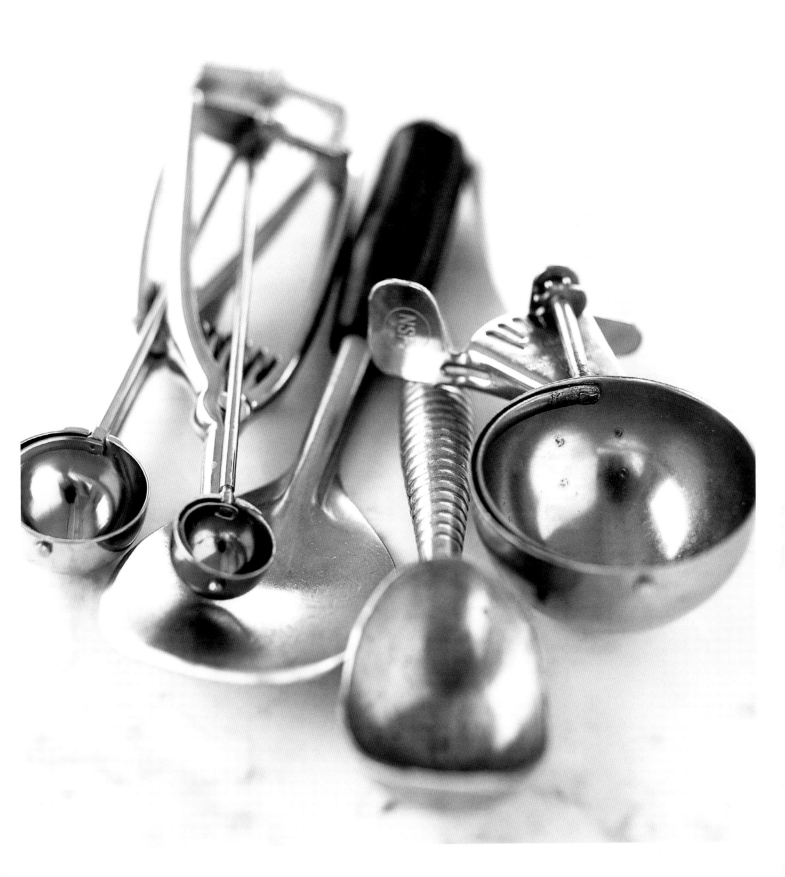

pans) as they can be used for thin cakes or cookies. A 9-inch round cake pan with sides 3 inches high is nice for tall one-layer and ice cream cakes.

Parchment paper: I would have a hard time baking without this. It makes baking and cleanup much simpler. Sift dry ingredients onto parchment paper. Pick up the parchment paper, forming a chute, and add the ingredients to another bowl without spilling.

Pastry bags: Disposable or canvas piping bags are frequently used in dessert making. A resealable plastic bag can be substituted if the task is not too precise. Cut and pipe from one of the bottom corners. You can get disposable bags at cookware and cake decorating stores. Avoid really small bags, as they don't hold much, and overfilled bags are more difficult and messier to pipe with.

Pie plates: Use glass or aluminum, whichever you prefer. Basic pie pans range in size from 9 to 10 inches. I like the wider pans as they are usually deeper as well, giving you more pie per piece.

Popsicle molds: Most Popsicle molds hold about 3½ ounces of liquid for each Popsicle. They come 8 or 10 per mold. Recipes may be easily scaled up or down to adjust to the number of Popsicles in the mold. Extra wooden sticks can be purchased at cookware and craft stores.

Scale, digital: A digital scale is best for accuracy, easy to read, and will become indispensable in your general cooking. Purchase one with a large enough base so you can still see the measurements when the bowl is on it.

Sieves, fine and medium mesh: For straining ice cream bases and fruit purées for sorbets. When straining berry purées, I often use a medium-mesh sieve and then a fine-mesh one. The medium mesh lets the liquid pass through quickly and gets some of the seeds, and the fine-mesh sieve gets rid of the remaining seeds.

Silicone bakeware: The newest thing in baking equipment, silicone molds can be used in both the oven and the freezer. They work exceptionally well for ice cream cakes, as they are flexible and make unmolding easy.

Silpat sheets: Pastry chefs have been using these flexible silicone mats for years. Now home cooks can too, as they are made to fit home-sized baking sheets. They provide a nonstick surface and can be washed and reused. They can be used in the place of parchment paper to line baking pans and for chocolate and caramel pieces.

Soda siphons: If you don't like lugging seltzer water home from the store, get one of these. They instantly turn regular tapwater into seltzer for sodas and floats. They come in brushed aluminum or bright colors (see Sources).

Spatulas: Heat-resistant silicone, plastic, and wooden spatulas are key in ice cream making. Use them when making custard bases to scrape the bottom of the pan thoroughly so the eggs won't scramble and the cream and milk won't burn. Plastic spatulas are best for mixing and folding ingredients and getting the last ingredients out of a bowl. But they are slicker than wood, so custard doesn't coat them as well, making it more difficult to tell when the custard is thick enough. Metal offset spatulas are good for layering and evenly spreading ice cream or sorbet in cakes, especially ones that are small enough to fit inside the pan.

Stand mixer: Although one of these is not needed for ice cream, unless you have the ice cream maker attachment to the KitchenAid mixer, this heavy-duty mixer and its paddle attachment are great for softening ice cream to mold it into a pan. The stand mixers are wonderful for baking.

Stove tops: Gas is my first choice, as you can see the size of the flame and can change it quickly. Electric burners take longer to regulate the temperature. If you are using an electric stove and your heat is too high, remove the pan for a minute to let the coils cool down and eliminate the risk of burning whatever is in your pan.

Thermometer, instant read: Many people shy away from thermometers, thinking they are too scientific, but in ice cream making they are indispensable. They take the guesswork out of knowing when a custard is thick enough. Digital thermometers are easier to read and tend to be more accurate.

Whisks: There are many shapes and sizes of whisks. Find one that is comfortable in your hand and not too stiff. You should have a 6-inch and a 9-inch whisk (measuring without the handle) for mixing varying quantities.

tips on making
frozen desserts

ice cream and sorbet bases

A custard ice cream base should be cooked to 175°F in order to yield a good-textured ice cream. This also ensures that the eggs are cooked enough to prevent salmonella.

Cool a hot ice cream base in an ice bath: Put 2 to 3 cups of ice cubes in a bowl and add water to cover. Put the ice cream base in a smaller bowl and set it in the ice bath. This chills the base faster and improves the texture. Ice cream bases should then be refrigerated for at least 4 hours, and sorbet bases should be chilled for at least 2 hours. They can be refrigerated as long as 2 days. Colder bases freeze faster, which improves their texture.

If a recipe calls for more than one ice cream and/or sorbet, you can make the bases at the same time. This lets you get all the cooking (and cleaning) finished at one time. You can then focus on churning.

When making ice creams, sorbets, and granitas, you don't have to use picture-perfect fruit. In fact, very ripe fruit works wonderfully. It may not look pretty enough for the top of a tart or to serve in a shortcake, but when puréed or mashed it will be delicious. Do make sure, however, that your fruit is not bruised or moldy. Underripe fruit does not have enough flavor for ice cream.

Candies are delicious to add to ice cream. They can either be chopped and sprinkled on top of the ice cream just before serving or mixed in after freezing and before hardening. Test how your candy choice freezes before you mix it into your ice cream by putting some candy pieces in the freezer to see how hard they get. You don't want them to freeze rock hard, or they will be difficult to eat. They should still be a little chewy.

When swirling ingredients into freshly churned ice cream, put the swirling ingredients in a bowl large enough to hold the ice cream and prefreeze for about 30 minutes. Put the freshly churned ice cream on top. Fold everything together and freeze until scoopable.

When straining purées, use the back of a small ladle (about ¼ cup) to push the liquid through the sieve. It is much quicker than using a rubber spatula.

Cooking fruit before adding it to a base brings out its flavor and reduces the water content, making the ice cream or sorbet less likely to be icy.

Keep in mind that finished ice creams and sorbets will not be as intensely flavored as the flavor of the bases. Cold temperatures mute flavor.

If you don't think your homemade ice cream has enough flavor, let it melt in the refrigerator, adjust the flavorings, and refreeze.

Watery juices like orange and pineapple make harder sorbets than thicker fruits like berries or mangoes. Add alcohol or more sugar to soften a hard sorbet, and add water to dilute a strong one. Some people add egg white, but it creates a fluffier sorbet.

storing ice cream and sorbet

Place a piece of parchment or waxed paper directly on the surface of the ice cream and then cover it with a tight-fitting lid or wrap the container well with plastic wrap. This will reduce the formation of ice crystals and prevent odors from spoiling the ice cream.

Don't store ice cream in the freezer door. It's not cold enough.

When an ice cream or sorbet finishes churning in the machine, it can be eaten right away. This is actually when it tastes the absolute best. It is, however, not hard enough to form a nice-looking scoop. If you want it scoopable, ice cream must be put in the freezer for about 4 hours and sorbet for about 2. This is called *hardening,* or *ripening,* the ice cream. The length of time required depends on your freezer. Frozen treats that have been formed in pans and require slicing need to be hard, not just scoopable. Know your freezer and plan accordingly.

Every time you take ice cream out of the freezer to scoop it, the texture of any remaining ice cream changes. It is best to put ice cream in several small containers so it isn't in and out of the freezer a bunch of times. I like plastic containers with tight-fitting lids.

Ice cream made in a White Mountain machine can be hardened right in the bucket if you are serving it within 2 hours. Fill the bucket with ice, add a little more salt than if you were freezing it, and cover the bucket with newspapers. There's no need to transfer the ice cream into another container or find room in the freezer.

serving ice cream

The correct portion size of ice cream depends on whether it will be served alone or as part of a dessert. It also depends on the size of your appetite.

Since homemade ice cream has no stabilizers, for best flavor and texture it should be eaten within 2 to 3 days. This is especially true with alcohol-flavored ice cream. Taste the ice cream at twenty-four- or even twelve-hour intervals, and you will notice the difference.

This may sound strange, but you should warm up your ice cream before serving it. Ice cream served immediately from the freezer can be difficult to scoop and isn't as flavorful as when it is a little warmer. Put it in the refrigerator for 10 minutes or so to soften it slightly. This is called *tempering*. When ice cream is too cold, the flavors are muted.

Dip ice cream scoops in cold water before scooping. This will allow for a cleaner, neater scoop. Warm water makes the ice cream too soft.

Restaurants often shape their ice creams and sorbets into a *quenelle*, an egg-shaped scoop with slightly pointed ends. To make a quenelle, run a large tablespoon under very hot water (it is important to have a wet spoon, or the quenelle will stick to the spoon). With the side of the spoon, pull a heaping scoop of ice cream toward you against the side of the container. When the spoon is full of ice cream, turn the spoon several times to shape the ice cream into an oval. Rewet your spoon to get a nice shape and allow the ice cream to release easily.

It's fun to collect pitchers for sauces, ice cream bowls, dishes for garnishes, and tall glasses for sodas and milk shakes. Start going to antiques and consignment shops, and you will have a new pastime. Sometimes I buy things for myself and end up giving them away later as gifts, or vice versa: I purchase something for a friend and then end up keeping it!

dessert-making tips

Read the recipe ahead of time to familiarize yourself with it. This eliminates any surprises and lets you understand what is required. Dessert preparation will be more relaxing if you know the sequence of steps.

Don't try new recipes when you are harried. Attempting anything new requires concentration, and unless you are focused you are setting yourself up for failure. This leads to frustration, which is not what dessert making is supposed to be about. Take your time with a new recipe. After you make something several times, your speed will improve. At first, focus on technique and on executing the recipe properly.

Many ingredients can be measured accurately in relatively small amounts using cups and tablespoons. Some foods, like chocolate, should always be weighed. Chocolate volume varies widely depending on how finely or roughly it is chopped.

Do not rely on the butter wrapper markings to measure your butter in tablespoons. Often the paper is not positioned properly. Each stick of butter is 4 ounces. It is simple to divide a stick in half for 2 ounces, into quarters for 1 ounce, and so on. An ounce of butter is equal to 4 tablespoons. Weigh your butter if you do not feel confident cutting it by sight.

melting chocolate: Fill the bottom of a double boiler one-third to one-quarter full of water. Bring the water to a boil. Finely chop the chocolate and place it in the top part of the double boiler. (You can make a double boiler by using a stainless-steel bowl and a saucepan with about 2 inches of water.) Turn off the heat and place the chocolate over the water. The bottom of the chocolate container should not touch the water. There will be enough residual heat to melt the chocolate. Let sit for several minutes and then stir.

measuring accurately: One of the biggest mistakes I see home cooks make is overpacking flour and sugar measures. To measure, dip a measuring cup into the sugar container to overflowing. With a knife, scrape off the excess so the sugar is even with the top. Measure flour in the same way, but first stir the flour to aerate it. Do not tap the full measuring cup on the counter or press the sugar or flour into the container with your fingers or a spoon. If you prefer to weigh your ingredients, 1 cup of sugar weighs 7 ounces and 1 cup of all-purpose flour weighs 5 ounces.

filling a pastry bag: Put the tip in the bag (if you are using a disposable piping bag or a new canvas bag, first cut off the end of the bag). Fold the top 2 inches of the bag over itself. If the mixture you are putting into the bag is thin, fold the bottom couple of inches of the bag and tip it upright to keep the ingredients from running out the bag. Place the bag in a tall glass or glass measuring cup (for a large bag, use a blender, a tall measuring container, or a vase). Fill the bag about two-thirds full. Do not overfill, or it will be difficult to pipe. Unfold the edges of the bag and twist it shut.

using a pastry bag: If you are right-handed, place the twisted top of the bag between the thumb and forefinger of your right hand and hold the top of the bag with your right hand. With your left hand, lightly hold the bag at the tip to steady it. With the fingers of your right hand, press the bag and the mixture will come out. Squeezing with the top hand provides even pressure and keeps air out of the bag. When you are finished piping the shape, stop pressing and then lift the bag slightly. Fast piping takes a little practice. Whip some egg whites and sugar and pipe until you get the hang of it. In no time at all you will be piping like a professional.

Sometimes all it takes to transform a few scoops of something frozen into an extraordinary dessert is an ingenuous twist. Some of the best frozen desserts are the simplest. Minimalist in appearance, these recipes burst with flavor. Add chocolate-covered pretzels to vanilla ice cream and serve fondue style with warm chocolate–peanut butter sauce and you have a new dessert for your chocoholic friends. Freeze the components of the famed Bellini cocktail for a light, refreshing end-of-the-meal treat. Expand on the traditional sundae theme with new ingredients such as crunchy meringue layered in whipped cream, or a little rose water added to raspberry sorbet, for a unique and phenomenal dessert. Combine any fresh fruit with ice cream or sorbet of a complementary flavor, as in Blackberry Sorbet–Filled Peaches or Lime Ice Cream with Blueberries and Sugared Mint Leaves, and you will have an exceptional dessert that couldn't be easier to prepare.

simply PRESENTED

black cow
sundaes

The precursor to this recipe is also known as a brown cow or a root beer float. It is made with root beer and ice cream and sometimes chocolate sauce. No matter what you call it, this float is a classic American dessert, a sweet little part of our history and culture. Kids slurp them down until they get brain freeze. Girls on stools at the ice cream counter sip root beer floats and bat their eyelashes at boys. Older folks enjoy the refreshing jolt of cold root beer and ice cream. This black cow recipe takes the same components and turns them inside out. The ice cream becomes the base, the root beer is made into a granita, and I put the chocolate sauce in the middle to make sure it is part of every bite.

SERVES
6

root beer granita

One 12-ounce bottle good-quality root beer

1 tablespoon sugar

½ teaspoon freshly squeezed lemon juice

⅛ teaspoon kosher salt

Bittersweet Chocolate Sauce, warmed (page 200)

French Vanilla Ice Cream (page 116) or Rich Vanilla Ice Cream (page 107)

TO MAKE THE GRANITA: In a medium bowl, stir together the root beer, sugar, lemon juice, and salt. Pour into a 9-inch square metal pan and freeze until solid, about 4 hours, depending on your freezer.

Break up the granita with a fork into light, feathery pieces. If it has been in the freezer overnight and is very hard, rap the pan of frozen granita on the counter to break it up and then put the granita in a food processor. Process until light and feathery. Cover and freeze in an airtight container until ready to serve.

TO ASSEMBLE THE SUNDAES: Place some chocolate sauce in the bottom of 6 glasses. Top with vanilla ice cream and a little more chocolate sauce. Place a heaping ½ cup granita over the ice cream. Serve immediately.

IN ADVANCE: The granita can be made 2 days in advance. The sundaes should be assembled just before serving.

blackberry sorbet–filled
peaches

A good summer peach is one whose juice dribbles through your fingers as you peel it. The juicier the peach, the sweeter and more succulent it will be. Peaches don't like to be cooked or refrigerated, because it dulls their aroma and taste. For maximum flavor, prepare them as simply as possible as in this easy-to-make dessert.

SERVES
6

blackberry sorbet

2 pints fresh or 24 ounces thawed no-sugar-added frozen blackberries

½ cup sugar, plus more if needed

½ cup water

2 teaspoons freshly squeezed lemon juice

⅛ teaspoon kosher salt

6 ripe freestone peaches

Chantilly Cream (page 205)

TO MAKE THE SORBET: Purée the blackberries in a food processor. Strain through a medium-mesh sieve, discarding the seeds. There should be about 2 cups purée. In a medium bowl, stir together the purée, the ½ cup sugar, the water, lemon juice, and salt. Taste and add more sugar if necessary. Refrigerate for at least 2 hours. Churn in an ice cream machine according to the manufacturer's instructions. Freeze until scoopable, about 2 hours, depending on your freezer.

TO SERVE: Peel and halve the peaches. Remove the pits. Slice a very thin piece off the bottom of 6 of the peach halves so the peaches will lie flat. Place a peach half, cut side down, on each of 6 plates. Place a large scoop of blackberry sorbet in the center of each of the halves. Cover with the second peach half, pressing gently together. Dollop some Chantilly cream on the side and serve immediately.

IN ADVANCE: Assemble the peaches just before serving.

flavor twist

biscotti ice cream (PAGE 69)
OR
cassis-berry sherbet (PAGE 109)
for the blackberry sorbet

chocolate cupcakes
stuffed with
pistachio ice cream

My fellow pastry chef and good friend Janet and I are constantly calling each other to bounce dessert ideas off each other and for general pastry 911 assistance. Our discussions can get quite analytical, due to the scientific nature of baking. But when it comes to critiquing a finished recipe like this one that we both fell in love with, our vocabulary is much simpler and comes down to one word—*yum.*

MAKES
6
LARGE CUPCAKES

pistachio ice cream
1 cup milk

2¼ cups heavy (whipping) cream

1¼ cups (5½ ounces) unsalted pistachios, toasted, skinned, and coarsely chopped (see pages 17–18), plus 2 tablespoons for garnish (optional)

5 large egg yolks

¾ cup granulated sugar

¼ teaspoon kosher salt

chocolate cupcakes
½ cup cake flour

½ cup all-purpose flour

⅓ cup unsweetened cocoa powder, preferably Dutch processed

1½ teaspoons baking soda

¼ teaspoon kosher salt

1 large egg

½ cup firmly packed dark brown sugar

½ cup granulated sugar

½ cup buttermilk

½ cup brewed coffee

⅓ cup canola oil

TO MAKE THE ICE CREAM: In a medium, heavy saucepan, cook the milk, cream, and all but 2 tablespoons of the pistachios over medium heat, stirring occasionally, until almost simmering. Turn off the heat, cover the pan, and let the pistachios steep in the cream for 15 minutes. In a medium bowl, whisk together the egg yolks, ¼ cup of the sugar, and the salt. Add the remaining ½ cup sugar to the pistachio cream and stir until dissolved. Slowly pour the cream into the eggs, whisking as you pour. Return the mixture to the pan and cook over medium-low heat, stirring constantly with a heat-resistant plastic or wooden spatula, until the mixture reaches 175°F and lightly coats the spatula. Cool over an ice bath and refrigerate for at least 4 hours or up to overnight. Strain the mixture into a clean bowl, discarding the pistachios. Churn in an ice cream machine according to the manufacturer's instructions. Freeze until scoopable, about 4 hours, depending on your freezer.

TO MAKE THE CUPCAKES: Preheat the oven to 350°F. Grease the insides of 6 large (about 3½ inches in diameter) muffin cups. Sift the cake and all-purpose flours, cocoa powder, and baking soda together onto a piece of parchment paper or into a bowl. Stir in the salt. In a large bowl, whisk together the egg and the brown and granulated sugars. In a small bowl, mix together the buttermilk, coffee, and canola oil. In 3 additions, alternately stir the wet and dry ingredients into the eggs. Divide the batter among the muffin cups. Bake until a skewer inserted in the center of a cupcake comes out clean, 15 to 20 minutes. Cool on a wire rack for 15 minutes. Carefully remove the cupcakes from the cups by running a knife around the inside edge of the cup. Let cool completely. Using a small knife, gently cut and remove enough of the inside of each cupcake so there is room for a scoop of ice cream. (Feel free to nibble on the scraps.)

continued

chocolate frosting

1 ounce bittersweet chocolate, chopped

2 ounces unsweetened chocolate, chopped

2 ounces (4 tablespoons) unsalted butter, softened

¾ cup confectioners' sugar

Large pinch of kosher salt

⅓ cup milk

flavor twist

caramel ice cream (PAGE 90)

OR

chocolate-covered-pretzel ice cream (PAGE 50)

TO MAKE THE FROSTING: Melt the bittersweet and unsweetened chocolates and 1 ounce (2 tablespoons) of the butter in a double boiler over very hot water. Stir until smooth.

Sift the confectioners' sugar into a large bowl and stir in the salt and milk. Stir in the melted chocolate and melted butter, mixing until well combined. Add the remaining 1 ounce (2 tablespoons) butter in 4 pieces, completely mixing in each piece before adding another. Stir until smooth. Let the frosting sit at room temperature until spreadable, about 2 hours. (If your kitchen is warm, you may have to briefly put the frosting in the refrigerator. Do not leave the frosting in the refrigerator too long or it will get too hard and a little grainy.) Stir occasionally to keep smooth.

TO ASSEMBLE THE CUPCAKES: Place a cupcake on each of 6 plates. Fill the holes with a scoop of the pistachio ice cream. Pipe or spread frosting on the cupcake around the ice cream, and sprinkle with the remaining 2 tablespoons pistachios, if you wish. Serve immediately.

IN ADVANCE: The cupcakes and frosting can be made 1 day ahead. Store separately, well wrapped in plastic wrap, at room temperature. Assemble the cupcakes just before serving.

bountiful berry compote
with buttermilk ice cream

In warm weather, I like to make great-tasting desserts but I want to spend less time in the kitchen doing it. I prefer enjoying the cool breezes of our screened porch while my husband whips me at Scrabble, or sinking into my wicker rocking chair with a novel. So I developed a standby simple dessert that is still dazzling, aromatic, and delicious. I like to pass both the ice cream and the compote in large bowls so people can serve themselves. Guests who are watching their waistlines can portion themselves lots of berries and a little ice cream, and the rest can be as liberal with a scoop as they dare.

SERVES
8

buttermilk ice cream
6 large egg yolks

¾ cup sugar

⅛ teaspoon kosher salt

2 cups heavy (whipping) cream

2 cups buttermilk

berry compote
1 cup freshly squeezed orange juice

1 teaspoon freshly squeezed lemon juice

2 tablespoons sugar

Large pinch of kosher salt

1 pint fresh strawberries, hulled and quartered if small, cut into eighths if large

2 ounces (4 tablespoons) unsalted butter, softened

½ pint fresh raspberries

1 pint fresh blackberries

flavor twist

mascarpone ice cream (PAGE 103)
OR
raspberry sorbet (PAGE 135)

TO MAKE THE ICE CREAM: Whisk together the egg yolks, ¼ cup of the sugar, and the salt in a medium bowl. In a heavy saucepan, cook the cream and remaining ½ cup sugar over medium heat, stirring occasionally, until almost simmering. Slowly pour the cream into the eggs, whisking as you pour. Return the mixture to the pan and cook over medium-low heat, stirring constantly with a heat-resistant plastic or wooden spatula until it reaches 175°F and lightly coats the spatula. Strain the custard into a clean bowl. Place over an ice bath and cool to room temperature. Stir in the buttermilk. Refrigerate for at least 4 hours or up to overnight. Churn in an ice cream machine according to the manufacturer's instructions. Freeze until scoopable, about 4 hours, depending on your freezer.

TO MAKE THE COMPOTE: Put the orange and lemon juices, sugar, and salt in a large sauté pan. Cook over medium-high heat, stirring occasionally, until the sugar has dissolved and the liquid reduces slightly, about 2 minutes. Add the strawberries and butter, gently stirring until the butter is almost completely melted, about 2 minutes. Add the raspberries and blackberries and continue to cook just until the raspberries and blackberries are warm, about 30 seconds. Do not overcook, or the berries will break apart.

TO SERVE: Scoop some buttermilk ice cream into bowls and spoon the berries and some sauce over the top. Or, separately pass the ice cream and compote in two large bowls. Serve immediately.

IN ADVANCE: The berry compote should be made just before serving.

caramelized apple and butter pecan **ice cream sundaes**

Don't be fooled by a sundae's simplicity. It is a magnificent dessert. A sundae may be only ice cream covered with sundry sauces and garnishes, but the variations are endless. In this refined interpretation of the traditional favorite, I coat apple pieces with sugar, bake them until they caramelize, and layer them with butter pecan ice cream and an apple sauce.

SERVES
• • • • 6 • • • •

butter pecan ice cream
4 large egg yolks

¼ cup firmly packed brown sugar

¾ cup granulated sugar

4 ounces (8 tablespoons) unsalted butter

2¾ cups milk

1¾ cups heavy (whipping) cream

1 cup (4½ ounces) pecan halves, halved lengthwise and toasted (see page 17)

apple sauce
2½ cups apple juice

6 tablespoons granulated sugar

caramelized apples
3 red-skinned apples, preferably Braeburn, Gala, or Fuji

¾ cup granulated sugar

TO MAKE THE ICE CREAM: Whisk the egg yolks, brown sugar, and ¼ cup of the granulated sugar together until smooth in a medium bowl. Cook the butter in a heavy saucepan over medium heat until light brown in color. Strain and slowly whisk it into the egg yolks.

Cook the remaining ½ cup granulated sugar, the milk, and cream in another heavy saucepan over medium heat, stirring occasionally, until almost simmering. Slowly pour the cream mixture into the eggs, whisking as you pour. Return the mixture to the saucepan. Cook over medium-low heat, stirring constantly with a heat-resistant plastic or wooden spatula, until the custard reaches 175°F and lightly coats the spatula.

Strain the custard into a clean bowl and cool over an ice bath until room temperature. Refrigerate for at least 4 hours or up to overnight. Churn in an ice cream machine according to the manufacturer's instructions. Stir in the pecans. Freeze the ice cream until scoopable, about 4 hours, depending on your freezer.

TO MAKE THE SAUCE: Stir together the apple juice and sugar in a heavy saucepan. Cook over medium heat until reduced to just under 1 cup. Let cool, then cover and refrigerate until cold.

TO MAKE THE APPLES: Preheat the oven to 400°F. Put a baking pan in the oven. Peel the apples, cut them in half, and remove the core. Cut the apples into 1-inch pieces. Mix them in a bowl with the sugar. Remove the pan from the oven and spread the apples on the pan in a single layer. Return the pan to the oven and cook the apples, gently mixing with a metal spatula after 10 minutes and then every 5 minutes, until caramelized, about 25 minutes. As you stir the apples, coat them with the liquid in the pan.

flavor twist

· · · · · · · · · · ·

cinnamon ice cream (PAGE 166)
OR
crème fraîche ice cream (PAGE 83)

TO ASSEMBLE THE SUNDAES: Scoop some butter pecan ice cream into 6 bowls. Spoon some sauce over the ice cream. Top with more ice cream and then warm apples. Pour more sauce over the top of the sundae. Serve immediately.

IN ADVANCE: The apple sauce can be made up to 1 week in advance. The apples are best made and served the same day. If you are not going to serve the apples right after you bake them, leave them on the pan and store at room temperature. Reheat in a preheated 350°F oven for 5 minutes.

cherries jubilee
with butter crunch ice cream

SERVES
6

For our thirteenth birthday, my parents surprised my twin brother, Allen, and me with a trip to New York City. Being country kids, we were thrilled at the dizzying excitement of the big city. We hailed our first cabs, saw the Empire State Building, and marveled at the life-sized stuffed animals at FAO Schwartz. Among our many firsts in New York was our first fine-dining experience; I can still see the brilliant cut-crystal glasses, the shimmering chandeliers, the elegant silverware, and the white linen tablecloths. My brother ordered cherries jubilee because he wanted to see the fruit on fire as they flambéed the cherries tableside. In grave tones, the waiter informed him that the sauce contained alcohol and was not served to minors. My father stepped in and Allen was able to live out his dream. I think cherries jubilee is even dreamier with a scoop of butter crunch ice cream.

butter crunch ice cream

3 cups heavy (whipping) cream

1 cup milk

⅓ cup plus ¾ cup sugar

⅛ teaspoon kosher salt

1 teaspoon vanilla extract

1 ounce (2 tablespoons) unsalted butter

¼ cup (1 ounce) walnuts, toasted and coarsely chopped (see page 17)

cherries

1½ pounds fresh Bing cherries

¾ cup freshly squeezed orange juice

6 tablespoons kirsch

2 tablespoons sugar

Large pinch of kosher salt

1½ ounces (3 tablespoons) unsalted butter

TO MAKE THE ICE CREAM: Cook the cream, milk, the ⅓ cup sugar, and the salt in a medium saucepan over medium heat, stirring occasionally, until almost simmering. Pour into a clean bowl and cool over an ice bath until room temperature. Stir in the vanilla extract. Refrigerate for 4 hours or up to overnight.

While the cream is in the refrigerator, prepare the butter crunch: Spray a 9-inch square baking pan with nonstick cooking spray. Melt the butter in a small saucepan over medium heat. Add the ¾ cup sugar and stir together. It will be very grainy. Cook over medium-low heat until the mixture becomes golden brown, about 5 minutes. Stir until the butter is mostly incorporated and the sugar is no longer grainy. Remove the pan from the heat, stir in the nuts, and then spread the mixture in the prepared pan. Let harden at room temperature, about 15 minutes. Drop the pan on the counter to coarsely break up the butter crunch. Chop medium fine in a food processor. Put the butter crunch in a medium bowl and put the bowl in the freezer.

Churn the vanilla ice cream base in an ice cream machine according to the manufacturer's instructions. Fold the ice cream into the butter crunch. Freeze until scoopable, about 4 hours, depending on your freezer.

flavor twist
. . . .

almond ice cream (PAGE 152)
OR
vin santo ice cream (PAGE 55)

TO MAKE THE CHERRIES: Stem and pit the cherries. In a large sauté pan, stir together the cherries, orange juice, kirsch, sugar, and salt. Cook over medium-high heat for about 3 minutes until the liquid is hot. Flambé the liquid by carefully touching a lighted long match to the liquid. The alcohol will catch on fire, burn for a minute, and then go out. (If you need to extinguish the flame, place a lid on top of the pan.) Add the butter and continue to cook for about 2 minutes, gently shaking the pan until the butter has melted.

TO SERVE: Scoop some ice cream into each of 6 bowls. Spoon some cherries and sauce over the ice cream. Serve immediately.

IN ADVANCE: The cherries can be pitted several hours in advance. They should be cooked just before serving.

crushed-meringue sundaes
with raspberry–rose water
sorbet and vanilla cream

Najmieh Batmangili is an Iranian cookbook author specializing in Persian food. Her generous spirit and love for her culture are inspiring. At a Culinary Institute of America at Greystone conference, she brought in a rose-water distiller so we could see firsthand how rose petals are miraculously transformed into rose water. To make rose water, damask roses (rosas de Castilla in Latin American countries) are picked before sunrise when their scent is at its peak. They are set out in a cool room before being steamed in a cauldron. The rose vapor is directed into a second pot, along with cold water, to produce the rose water. The leftover petals are not wasted; some are combined with tobacco and smoked, while others are fed to goats and cows, creating rose-scented milk. Any petals that remain are reused as fertilizer for the rosebushes. (See Sources, page 216 for rose water.) Inspired by Najmieh, I came home and developed this recipe.

SERVES
8

raspberry–rose water sorbet
4 pints fresh or 48 ounces thawed no-sugar-added frozen raspberries

1⅓ cups sugar

⅓ cup water

1 tablespoon freshly squeezed lemon juice

⅛ teaspoon kosher salt

1 teaspoon rose water

meringue
2 large egg whites

½ cup sugar

vanilla cream
1 vanilla bean, halved lengthwise

2½ cups heavy (whipping) cream

½ pint fresh raspberries

TO MAKE THE SORBET: Purée the raspberries in a food processor. Strain the purée through a sieve into a bowl, discarding the seeds. There should be about 4 cups purée. Stir together the raspberry purée, sugar, water, lemon juice, salt, and rose water. Refrigerate for at least 2 hours or up to overnight. Churn in an ice cream machine according to the manufacturer's instructions. Freeze until scoopable, about 2 hours, depending on your freezer.

TO MAKE THE MERINGUE: Preheat the oven to 200°F. Line a 9-inch square baking pan with parchment paper. With an electric mixer, whip the egg whites on medium speed until frothy. Increase to medium-high speed and slowly add half of the sugar. Whip until stiff, glossy peaks form, about 5 minutes. Fold in the remaining sugar. Spread the meringue into the prepared pan. Bake until dry, 1 to 2 hours. Let cool to room temperature. Run a knife around the inside edge of the pan. Invert the meringue and the pan onto a cutting board and remove the pan. Peel off the parchment paper and break the meringue into ¾-inch pieces.

TO MAKE THE VANILLA CREAM: Scrape the seeds out of the vanilla bean. Put the seeds (reserve the bean for another use) and cream in a bowl and whisk until soft peaks form. Fold in three-fourths of the meringue.

continued

flavor twist

blood orange sorbet (PAGE 165)

OR

plum sorbet (PAGE 181)

TO ASSEMBLE THE SUNDAES: Divide half of the meringue cream among 8 sundae glasses. Place some sorbet in the glasses and cover with the remaining crushed-meringue cream. Garnish with the remaining meringue pieces and fresh raspberries. Serve immediately.

IN ADVANCE: If it is not humid outside, the meringues can be made several days in advance. Store in an airtight container. The vanilla cream can be made up to 4 hours in advance. Cover with plastic wrap and refrigerate. If necessary, rewhip slightly before serving. Add the meringue pieces to the cream just before assembling the sundaes.

ICE CREAM SHOP

profile

Toscanini's

899 MAIN STREET &
1310 MASSACHUSETTS AVENUE
CAMBRIDGE, MASSACHUSETTS

MOTTO: "The Best Ice Cream in the World."

YEAR OPENED: 1981.

OWNER: Gus Rancatore.

HOW THE NAME WAS CHOSEN: Gus's former partner's grandfather played with Toscanini.

NUMBER OF FLAVORS IN REPERTOIRE: Eighty-five to ninety; including frozen yogurt, sorbet, and gelato. The selection offered depends on the store; the Main Street shop in Central Square is bigger.

MOST POPULAR FLAVORS: Nocciola, coffee, Belgian chocolate, French vanilla, burnt caramel, mango.

SIGNATURE FLAVORS: Molasses ginger, cocoa pudding, Guinness, Grape Nuts with raisins.

WHAT THEY DO WHEN IT GETS COLD OUT: Turn on the heat inside the shop. Sales don't dip as much as you would think.

AVAILABLE FOR SHIPPING: No, you'll have to go there.

THE SCOOP: Gus started making ice cream with two White Mountain ice cream machines in an eight-hundred-square-foot shop.

arnold palmer ice
with blueberries and raspberries

Walk up to a bartender and order lemonade and iced tea, and you will be presented with what is known as an Arnold Palmer. Beverage companies sell a refreshing bottled drink of lemonade and iced tea called Half and Half. Churn this mixture in an ice cream machine and serve it frozen and it is even better. On a sticky, blistering day, this slightly tart ice cools you from the inside out. If the base is a little too puckery for you, add another tablespoon or two of sugar before freezing.

SERVES
6

arnold palmer ice

3 cups water

1 tablespoon English Breakfast or other black tea leaves

7 tablespoons sugar

½ cup freshly squeezed lemon juice

Large pinch of kosher salt

½ pint fresh blueberries
½ pint fresh raspberries

TO MAKE THE ICE: In a medium saucepan, bring 1½ cups of the water to a boil. Turn off the heat, add the tea, cover, and let steep for 5 minutes. Strain the tea, discarding the tea leaves, into a bowl. Stir in the sugar and let cool to room temperature. Stir in the lemon juice, the remaining 1½ cups water, and the salt. Refrigerate until cold, about 2 hours or up to overnight. Churn in an ice cream machine according to the manufacturer's instructions. For a smoother texture, freeze until scoopable, about 2 hours. For an icier texture, freeze until hard, 6 hours to overnight, and break it up with the end of a spoon or the tines of a fork. In either case, serve in bowls with the berries.

IN ADVANCE: The ice can be made 2 days in advance.

dulce de leche frozen yogurt and chocolate sorbet
tartufos

I often create desserts that are takeoffs from one culture or another. This dessert, however, is truly a melting pot of culinary contributions. Tartufos are Italian in origin and reflect that country's love for truffles: gelato is served in a ball to resemble a truffle's shape, and ice cream is hidden in the center. Dulce de leche, a luscious caramelized milk sauce, is the national treat of Argentina. It has recently captured the American sweet tooth as well. Frozen yogurt is the American contribution, a low-fat alternative to ice cream that still satisfies those sweet cravings. Combine these together in one dessert, and you have a winner all over the world.

SERVES
8

chocolate sorbet

¾ cup sugar

¼ cup unsweetened cocoa powder

1¾ cups water

½ cup milk

3 tablespoons corn syrup

4 ounces bittersweet chocolate, chopped

dulce de leche frozen yogurt

1 cup dulce de leche (see page 17)

1½ cups plain yogurt

¾ cup heavy (whipping) cream

¼ cup milk

⅛ teaspoon kosher salt

⅔ cup (3 ounces) hazelnuts, toasted and skinned (see pages 17–18)

½ cup chocolate sprinkles, preferably Guittard

Bittersweet Chocolate Sauce, warmed (page 200)

TO MAKE THE SORBET: Stir together the sugar and cocoa powder in a medium saucepan. Stir in the water, milk, and corn syrup. Bring to a boil over medium-high heat and cook for 3 minutes, stirring frequently once it comes to a boil. Remove from the heat and whisk in the chocolate until melted. Cool over an ice bath until room temperature. Refrigerate for 4 hours or up to overnight. Churn in an ice cream machine according to the manufacturer's instructions. Freeze until scoopable, about 2 hours, depending on your freezer.

TO MAKE THE FROZEN YOGURT: In a bowl, whisk together all the ingredients until well blended. Refrigerate for at least 2 hours or up to overnight. Churn in an ice cream machine according to the manufacturer's instructions. Freeze until scoopable, about 4 hours, depending on your freezer.

TO ASSEMBLE THE TARTUFOS: Grind the hazelnuts in a food processor. In a bowl, combine the hazelnuts with the chocolate sprinkles.

Scoop 8 large balls of the frozen yogurt and put them on a single layer on a baking sheet lined with plastic wrap. If they are soft, refreeze until firm. Using a scoop about 1½ inches in diameter, remove a scoop of frozen yogurt from each ball. Set the small balls aside. Working quickly, fill the hole with a scoop of the chocolate sorbet. Cover the sorbet with the reserved frozen yogurt balls. Again, refreeze the yogurt balls if they become too soft to work with.

coconut ice cream (PAGE 68)
AND
passion fruit ice cream (PAGE 178),
OR
peanut butter ice cream (PAGE 80)
AND
chocolate–chocolate chunk
ice cream (PAGE 183)

Place a plastic bag on each hand and press the hazelnut chocolate mixture around each of the ice cream balls; if necessary, shape into round balls. Freeze until firm, about 1 hour, depending on your freezer.

TO SERVE THE TARTUFOS: Pool the warm chocolate sauce on each plate. Place a tartufo on top. Serve immediately.

IN ADVANCE: The tartufos can be assembled 2 days in advance.

chocolate-covered-pretzel
ice cream ball fondue

My mother liked to serve meat fondue, on the theory that if you were required to cook your food and eat it at the table then everybody stayed longer and there was more family conversation. If she had made fondue with chocolate-covered-pretzel ice cream, we would have stayed and chatted until breakfast.

SERVES
8—10

chocolate-covered-pretzel ice cream

1 cup milk

2¼ cups heavy (whipping) cream

¾ cup sugar

5 large egg yolks

⅛ teaspoon kosher salt

2 ounces bittersweet chocolate, coarsely chopped

¾ cup ½-inch pretzel pieces

¾ cup (3½ ounces) coarsely chopped pecans or whole natural almonds, toasted (see page 17)

1 cup graham cracker or plain biscotti crumbs

Chocolate–Peanut Butter Sauce, warmed (page 202)

White Chocolate Sauce, warmed (page 199)

flavor twist

grand marnier ice cream (PAGE 185)
OR
penuche swirl ice cream (PAGE 96)

TO MAKE THE ICE CREAM: In a medium, heavy saucepan, cook the milk, cream, and ½ cup of the sugar over medium heat, stirring occasionally, until almost simmering. In a medium bowl, whisk together the egg yolks, the remaining ¼ cup sugar, and the salt. Slowly pour the cream into the eggs, whisking as you pour. Return the mixture to the pan. Cook over medium-low heat, stirring constantly with a heat-resistant plastic or wooden spatula, until the mixture reaches 175°F and lightly coats the spatula. Strain into a clean bowl and cool over an ice bath until room temperature. Refrigerate for at least 4 hours or up to overnight.

While the ice cream base is chilling, melt the chocolate in a double boiler over very hot water. Line a baking sheet with parchment paper. Remove the pan from the heat, stir in the pretzel pieces, and spread them in a single layer on the prepared pan. Let the chocolate harden, about 1 hour. Break the chocolate pretzel pieces into ¼-inch pieces. Put them in a medium bowl with the pecans and put the bowl in the freezer. Churn the ice cream base in an ice cream machine according to the manufacturer's instructions. Put the ice cream in the bowl with the pretzels and nuts and fold together. Freeze the ice cream until scoopable, about 4 hours, depending on your freezer.

Put the graham cracker crumbs in a bowl. Scoop the ice cream into balls with a scoop about 1½ inches in diameter. If the ice cream balls get soft, return them to the freezer to harden. Coat the ice cream balls with the crumbs, pressing the crumbs into the ice cream. Place in a single layer on a baking sheet. Refreeze until firm, about 1 hour.

TO SERVE THE FONDUE: Put the chocolate–peanut butter and white chocolate sauces in small attractive serving dishes on the table. Place the ice cream balls on a platter. Let guests dip the ice cream balls in the sauces to order.

IN ADVANCE: The ice cream balls can be formed a day or two in advance. Freeze in a single layer on a baking sheet. Wrap well in plastic wrap.

iced
bellinis

A frozen version of the famed Cipriani Bellini cocktail, this can be served as an aperitif on a hot summer night, as a mid-course palate cleanser, or as a light dessert. Coupe-style champagne glasses are perfect to serve this in. Since they are rarely used for drinking Champagne anymore, you can often find them at a flea market or a thrift shop, but a martini glass works well too. If you use a drier sparkling wine, you may have to increase the sugar a bit. Use white peaches if you can get them, but be sure to churn the sorbet right after you purée it or the purée will discolor.

SERVES
6

peach sorbet
3¼ pounds (about 8) ripe white or yellow peaches

½ cup sugar

1 teaspoon freshly squeezed lemon juice

Large pinch of kosher salt

sparkling wine granita
1¼ cups prosecco or other sparkling wine

3½ tablespoons granulated sugar

¾ cup water

1 large ripe white or yellow peach, peeled, pitted, and diced

TO MAKE THE SORBET: Peel and pit the peaches. Purée the peaches in a food processor until smooth. Strain the purée through a medium-mesh sieve into a medium bowl. Discard the pulp and skins. There should be 3 cups purée. Stir in the sugar, lemon juice, and salt. Churn in an ice cream machine according to the manufacturer's instructions. Freeze until scoopable, about 2 hours, depending on your freezer.

TO MAKE THE GRANITA: Stir the wine, sugar, and water together in a bowl until the sugar dissolves. Pour into a 9-by-13-inch pan and freeze for about 1 hour until it begins to harden. Stir the mixture with a fork and place it back in the freezer. Continue to freeze, stirring every 30 minutes, until frozen, about 4 hours, depending on your freezer. When frozen, the granita will have a light, feathery texture.

TO SERVE: Place small scoops of peach sorbet in 6 bowls. Spoon the granita over the sorbet. Garnish with the diced peaches. Serve immediately.

IN ADVANCE: The granita can be made a day or two in advance. The sorbet can be made a day in advance.

lime ice cream
with blueberries
and sugared mint leaves

For me, the beginning and end of summer are marked not by the calendar but by the size of the blueberry containers in the grocery store. In late June, as blueberries start to appear they are packed in half-pint containers. At the height of summer, they come in full-pint containers and only shrink again to the smaller size at the end of August. If you can find wild blueberries in your area, by all means use them instead of commercially grown ones. Although they are not as plump and won't produce as juicy a sauce, their flavor is exquisite. In either case, warming the blueberries heightens their flavor. Blueberries are frequently paired with lemon, but here for a change I use lime. After making this recipe, I now prefer it over lemon.

SERVES
6
• • • •   • • • •

lime ice cream
4 large egg yolks

¾ cup sugar

⅛ teaspoon kosher salt

2½ cups heavy (whipping) cream

1¼ cups milk

Grated zest of 3 limes

1 tablespoon freshly squeezed lime juice

sugared mint leaves
About 3 tablespoons sugar

1 egg white

18 fresh mint leaves

TO MAKE THE ICE CREAM: In a bowl, whisk together the egg yolks, ¼ cup of the sugar, and the salt. Combine the cream, milk, lime zest, and remaining ½ cup sugar in a heavy saucepan. Heat the cream and milk over medium heat, stirring occasionally, until almost simmering. Slowly pour the hot liquid into the egg-and-sugar mixture, whisking as you pour. Return the egg-and-cream mixture to the saucepan. Cook over medium-low heat, stirring constantly with a heat-resistant plastic or wooden spatula, until the custard reaches 175°F and lightly coats the spatula.

Strain the custard into a clean bowl, discarding the lime zest. Cool over an ice bath until room temperature. Stir in the lime juice. Refrigerate for 4 hours or up to overnight. Churn in an ice cream machine according to the manufacturer's instructions. Freeze for about 4 hours until scoopable, depending on your freezer.

TO MAKE THE MINT LEAVES: In a small bowl, lightly beat the egg white with a fork. Put the sugar in another small bowl. Using a pastry brush, very lightly brush both sides of a mint leaf with the egg white. Dip the leaf into the sugar, completely coating it. Place the mint leaf on a plate. Repeat with the remaining mint leaves, making sure they are not touching as you place them on the plate. Let sit at room temperature until dry, about 4 hours. Store in a single layer in an airtight container.

continued

blueberries

2 pints fresh blueberries

⅓ cup sugar

2 teaspoons freshly squeezed lemon juice

Pinch of kosher salt

flavor twist

. . . .

vanilla malt ice cream (PAGE 119)
OR
butter pecan ice cream (PAGE 40)

TO MAKE THE BLUEBERRIES: Put the blueberries, sugar, lemon juice, and salt in a medium saucepan. Cook over medium-low heat, stirring frequently, until the sugar dissolves and the berries begin to give off some of their juices.

TO SERVE THE DESSERT: Scoop some ice cream into each of 6 bowls. Spoon some blueberries on top and garnish with 3 sugared mint leaves per bowl. Serve immediately.

IN ADVANCE: The sugared mint leaves can be made 1 day ahead unless it is humid; in that case, they need to be made the same day. Store at room temperature. The blueberries can be prepared up to 2 days before serving. Keep refrigerated. Reheat gently before serving.

vin santo ice cream with **figs and almonds**

I love the taste of a rich vin santo dessert wine, but after a meal with wine and savory food, I often don't feel like drinking more alcohol. I get around that by sneaking this favorite wine into my dessert. In this recipe, the traditional Italian dessert of vin santo wine served with fresh figs is rearranged and served frozen. The original elements are still there, just presented in a new way. Vin santo is produced differently by each winery, so taste a few to find your favorite. You can serve the rest of the bottle with the dessert or cork it for another evening.

SERVES
6

vin santo ice cream
3 cups heavy (whipping) cream

1 cup milk

½ cup sugar

Large pinch of kosher salt

½ cup vin santo

fig-almond garnish
12 fresh Black Mission figs

1 cup (4½ ounces) whole natural almonds, toasted and coarsely chopped (see page 17)

2 tablespoons vin santo

TO MAKE THE ICE CREAM: Cook the cream, milk, and sugar in a heavy saucepan over medium-high heat, stirring occasionally, until almost simmering. Transfer to a bowl and cool over an ice bath until room temperature. Stir in the salt and vin santo. Refrigerate until cold, at least 4 hours or up to overnight. Churn in an ice cream machine according to the manufacturer's instructions. Freeze the ice cream until scoopable, about 4 hours, depending on your freezer.

TO MAKE THE GARNISH AND SERVE THE DESSERT: Stem the figs and cut them lengthwise into eighths. Scoop some ice cream into 6 bowls. Place some figs and almonds on top. Drizzle the vin santo over the top of the fruit and nuts. Serve immediately.

IN ADVANCE: The figs can be cut several hours in advance.

flavor twist
. . . .

cinnamon ice cream (PAGE 166)
OR
raspberry sorbet (PAGE 135)

pineapple–dark rum granita
with ginger beer sabayon and raspberries

SERVES
····· 8 ·····

It's difficult for me to write a dessert menu without using some variation of a sabayon. Rich and luscious without being heavy, sabayons are one of the finest of all dessert sauces. They can accompany cake, form an integral part of a dessert such as a trifle, or be a crucial component of a dessert, as here. The flavor possibilities are endless. Sparkling wine, dessert wines, or liqueurs such as Grand Marnier, Amaretto, or Frangelico can all be used as the liquid. If using a liqueur, combine one third of the liqueur with two thirds the amount of orange juice or it will be too sweet. Nonalcoholic versions can be made with sparkling apple cider, apple juice, or ginger beer (which is nonalcoholic).

pineapple–dark rum granita
1 pineapple, about 3¼ pounds

¼ cup sugar

2 tablespoons dark rum

Large pinch of kosher salt

ginger beer sabayon
4 large egg yolks

¼ cup sugar

Large pinch of kosher salt

6 tablespoons ginger beer

½ cup heavy (whipping) cream

1 pint fresh raspberries for serving

TO MAKE THE GRANITA: Remove the rind from the pineapple. From the top, cut into quarters and then cut out and discard the core. Cut the pineapple into 1-inch pieces. Purée the pineapple in a food processor. Strain through a medium-mesh sieve. Stir in the sugar, rum, and salt. Pour into a 9-by-13-inch pan and freeze for about 1 hour until it begins to harden. Stir the mixture with a fork and place it back in the freezer. Freeze, stirring every 30 minutes with a fork, until frozen, about 4 to 6 hours, depending on your freezer.

TO MAKE THE SABAYON: In a medium stainless-steel bowl, whisk together the egg yolks, sugar, and salt. Whisk in the ginger beer. Place the bowl over a saucepan with 2 inches of rapidly simmering water, making sure the water is not touching the bottom of the bowl. Whisk constantly until thick and ribbony, about 3 minutes. Place over an ice bath, stirring occasionally, and let cool to room temperature. Whip the cream to soft peaks. Fold the cream into the ginger beer mixture. Refrigerate until ready to serve.

TO SERVE THE GRANITA: Place some raspberries in the bottom of individual glasses or bowls. Top with a spoonful of sabayon and then fill the glass with granita. Dollop a little more sabayon on top. Serve immediately.

IN ADVANCE: The granita can be made a couple days in advance. Store in an airtight container. If it freezes solid, break it up with a fork. The sabayon can be made a day in advance. Keep refrigerated in an airtight container.

If eating ice cream is one of life's ultimate pleasures, eating it with your fingers must be close to heaven.

Think ice cream sandwich, and you think, *vanilla ice cream bookended by soft chocolate wafers.* Once again, I have been unable to leave tradition alone. After peanut butter ice cream between ranger cookies, coconut ice cream between coffee meringues, and mint chocolate chip ice cream between fudge cookies, sandwiches will never be the same.

I wrote extra cookies into every recipe, in case of breakage or, more likely, nibblage—these irresistible cookies tend to get bites taken out of them during preparation. Slightly soften the ice cream or sorbet when you assemble them so the cookies won't break when you press the sandwich together. Store in a single layer on a baking sheet in the freezer. Freeze until solid and then wrap them individually in plastic wrap to keep the flavors fresh.

These sandwiches make a great casual dessert, but don't stop there. Serve them individually on a plate with some sauce, a crunchy garnish, or some fresh fruit at the most formal dinner party. (In these cases, I would offer a spoon—it's less messy.)

Like your ice cream and sorbet straight up? All your favorites can be frozen onto sticks. Fill the molds immediately after churning. Milk Chocolate–Chocolate Chip Frozen Yogurt Sticks and Chocolate–Soy Milk Frozen Pops are perfect snacks when you crave an afternoon pick-me-up. Strawberry–Passion Fruit Popsicles show you the basics for making your own Popsicles. You barely need a recipe. Purée and strain the fruit and sweeten to taste. If the purée is thick, thin it out with a little water. Pour into molds and freeze. Dessert making never has been so fresh or easy.

with your FINGERS

chocolate-coated cocoa nib florentines
and orange ice cream sandwiches

Cocoa nibs are little pieces of shelled cocoa beans. They have been the most exciting new ingredient for pastry chefs in many years. When they first arrived, we went wild and tested them in all types of desserts—ice cream, cookies, candies; some even used them straight as a garnish. Thanks to Scharffen Berger Chocolate, they are now available in gourmet cookware stores and Whole Foods markets across the country. Since cocoa nibs are unsweetened, they do have a slightly bitter taste, but when combined with sweet ingredients they produce a wonderful contrast.

MAKES

12

SANDWICHES

orange ice cream
3 large egg yolks

½ cup sugar

⅛ teaspoon kosher salt

2¼ cups heavy (whipping) cream

¾ cup milk

Zest stripped from 2 oranges

1 tablespoon freshly squeezed orange juice

florentines
2 ounces (4 tablespoons) unsalted butter

¼ cup heavy (whipping) cream

6 tablespoons sugar

2 tablespoons plus ¾ teaspoon all-purpose flour

⅓ cup (1½ ounces) plus ¼ cup (1¼ ounces) pistachios, toasted, skinned, and chopped (see pages 17–18)

½ cup cocoa nibs

4 ounces bittersweet chocolate, melted

TO MAKE THE ICE CREAM: In a bowl, whisk together the egg yolks, ¼ cup of the sugar, and the salt in a bowl. Combine the cream, milk, orange zest, and remaining ¼ cup sugar in a heavy saucepan. Cook over medium heat, stirring occasionally, until almost simmering. Slowly pour the hot liquid into the egg-and-sugar mixture, whisking as you pour.

Return the egg-and-cream mixture to the saucepan. Cook over medium-low heat, stirring constantly with a heat-resistant plastic or wooden spatula, until the custard reaches 175°F and lightly coats the spatula. Cool over an ice bath until room temperature. Stir in the orange juice. Refrigerate the custard for at least 4 hours, or up to overnight. Strain the custard into a clean bowl, discarding the orange zest. Churn in an ice cream machine according to the manufacturer's instructions. Freeze until scoopable, about 4 hours, depending on your freezer.

TO MAKE THE FLORENTINES: Preheat the oven to 350°F. Line 3 baking sheets with parchment paper. Melt the butter in a saucepan over medium heat. Add the cream, sugar, flour, the ⅓ cup pistachios, and the cocoa nibs. Cook the mixture over medium-low heat, stirring constantly, until it thickens and comes clean from the bottom of the pan as you stir, about 3 minutes. Remove the pan from the heat.

Drop teaspoonfuls of the batter 3½ inches apart on the prepared pans. The cookies will spread as they bake. Bake until golden brown, about 10 minutes. Let the cookies cool to room temperature on the pans and then remove them with a metal spatula. You will need 24 cookies for the sandwiches.

continued

When cool, turn the Florentines over with an offset spatula and gently coat the bottoms with a thin layer of the melted chocolate, using a small pastry spatula. Let harden, about 10 minutes.

TO ASSEMBLE THE SANDWICHES: Place half of the Florentines chocolate side up. Place a scoop of ice cream on top. Gently, so as to not crack the cookies, press a second Florentine on top, adhering the sandwiches together. Place the ¼ cup of pistachios around the sides of the sandwiches. Serve immediately, or freeze until ready to serve.

IN ADVANCE: The Florentines can be made a day ahead. Coat them with the chocolate the day you assemble the sandwiches. Store the cookies in an airtight container. The sandwiches can be assembled 1 to 2 days in advance. Store wrapped in plastic wrap or in an airtight container.

chocolate–soy milk
frozen pops

Linger in a coffee shop for a few minutes and listen to the barista call out the orders. At least a quarter of them will be for soy lattes or cappuccinos. Soy milk is cholesterol-free, has lots of iron and protein, and is low in fat and sodium. It's a boon for the lactose intolerant. This recipe can also be enjoyed by those who are not big fans of soy milk, as the chocolate and cocoa powder masks some of the soy flavor. These taste like old-fashioned Fudgsicles.

4½ ounces bittersweet chocolate, finely chopped

3 cups soy milk

6 tablespoons sugar

6 tablespoons corn syrup

3 tablespoons canola oil

3 tablespoons unsweetened cocoa powder

¼ teaspoon kosher salt

TO MAKE THE POPS: Melt the chocolate in a double boiler over hot water and transfer to a medium bowl. In a separate bowl, whisk together the soy milk, sugar, corn syrup, and canola oil. Whisk in the cocoa powder and salt. Pour 1 cup of the soy milk mixture into the chocolate and whisk until smooth. Whisk in the remaining mixture.

Pour into Popsicle molds and put a stick in the center of each. Freeze until hard, about 8 hours, depending on your freezer. Unmold by running the molds briefly under hot water and then gently pulling on the sticks.

IN ADVANCE: The frozen pops can be made up to a week in advance. Once unmolded, wrap individually in plastic wrap.

brown sugar oat wafers
with candied ginger ice cream

MAKES

..... 12 .....

SANDWICHES

To get the best flavor for ginger ice cream, you have to work from both the inside and the outside. The milk and cream must be steeped with fresh ginger to give the ice cream a deep ginger taste. But add too much fresh ginger and the ice cream will be too spicy. Yet there is still room for more flavor. That's where candied ginger comes in. Folding in chopped pieces of candied ginger gives you a tiny jolt of ginger taste every couple of spoonfuls, which is enough to carry you through until you bite into the next one. The cookies for these sandwiches stay crunchy even when frozen. They can be a bit irregular in shape, but that's the beauty of homemade ice cream sandwiches: each one is unique. To transform this into a plated dessert, serve with Coffee Caramel Sauce (page 204).

candied ginger ice cream
1¾ cups heavy (whipping) cream

1½ cups milk

⅔ cup sugar

3-inch piece fresh ginger, cut into ½-inch pieces

7 large egg yolks

⅛ teaspoon kosher salt

½ cup finely chopped candied ginger

brown sugar oat wafers
1¼ ounces (2½ tablespoons) unsalted butter

¼ cup firmly packed brown sugar

2 tablespoons granulated sugar

2 tablespoons dark corn syrup

¾ cup old-fashioned rolled oats

TO MAKE THE ICE CREAM: Combine the cream, milk, ⅓ cup of the sugar, and the fresh ginger in a medium, heavy saucepan. Cook over medium heat, stirring occasionally, until almost simmering. Whisk together the egg yolks, the remaining ⅓ cup sugar, and the salt. Slowly pour the cream into the egg yolks, whisking as you pour. Return the mixture to the pan and cook, stirring constantly with a heat-resistant plastic or wooden spatula, over medium-low heat until the liquid reaches 175°F and lightly coats the spatula. Strain into a bowl, discarding the ginger, and cool over an ice bath to room temperature. Refrigerate for at least 4 hours or up to overnight.

Put the candied ginger in a bowl and put it in the freezer. Churn the chilled custard in an ice cream machine according to the manufacturer's instructions. Fold the ice cream and candied ginger together. Freeze until scoopable, about 4 hours, depending on your freezer.

TO MAKE THE WAFERS: Preheat the oven to 350°F. Line 3 baking sheets with parchment paper. In a medium saucepan, melt the butter over medium heat. Turn off the heat and add the brown and granulated sugars and the corn syrup, stirring until combined. Stir in the oats.

For each wafer, place ½ teaspoonfuls of the oat mixture 2 inches apart on the prepared pans. Bake until golden brown, about 10 minutes. The cookies will spread as they bake. Let the cookies cool to room temperature and then remove them from the pans with a metal spatula.

TO ASSEMBLE THE SANDWICHES: Place half of the oat crisps, bottom side up, in a single layer on parchment or waxed paper–lined baking sheets. Place a small scoop of ice cream on top of each. Cover with a second oat crisp and gently press down to adhere the sandwiches together. Serve immediately, or freeze until ready to serve.

IN ADVANCE: The cookies can be made and stored in an airtight container up to 2 days in advance. The sandwiches can be made a day ahead. Once frozen, wrap well in plastic wrap for up to 3 days.

ICE CREAM SHOP

profile

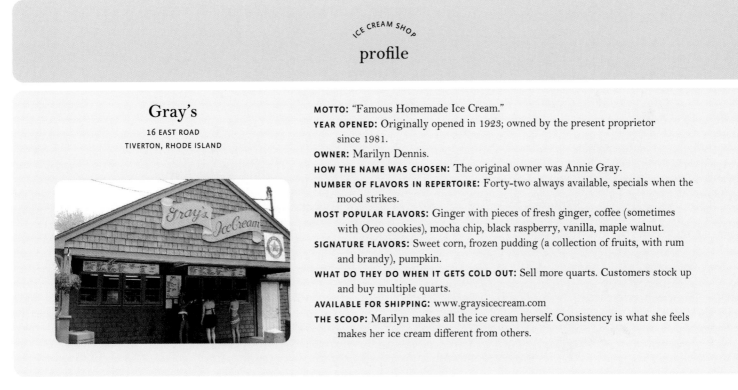

Gray's

16 EAST ROAD
TIVERTON, RHODE ISLAND

MOTTO: "Famous Homemade Ice Cream."

YEAR OPENED: Originally opened in 1923; owned by the present proprietor since 1981.

OWNER: Marilyn Dennis.

HOW THE NAME WAS CHOSEN: The original owner was Annie Gray.

NUMBER OF FLAVORS IN REPERTOIRE: Forty-two always available, specials when the mood strikes.

MOST POPULAR FLAVORS: Ginger with pieces of fresh ginger, coffee (sometimes with Oreo cookies), mocha chip, black raspberry, vanilla, maple walnut.

SIGNATURE FLAVORS: Sweet corn, frozen pudding (a collection of fruits, with rum and brandy), pumpkin.

WHAT DO THEY DO WHEN IT GETS COLD OUT: Sell more quarts. Customers stock up and buy multiple quarts.

AVAILABLE FOR SHIPPING: www.graysicecream.com

THE SCOOP: Marilyn makes all the ice cream herself. Consistency is what she feels makes her ice cream different from others.

coffee meringues
with coconut ice cream

Brainstorming for recipe ideas is one of the greatest pleasures of writing. I think them up while in the shower, washing the dishes, driving to work. It is a 24/7 engagement. Friends and family love to participate in this phase, offering some terrific and some rather bizarre combinations. My niece, Lauren, requested that I create something using coffee and coconut together. It's not something you see often, but it may quickly become one of your favorites. If you need a chocolate fix, these taste great with chocolate sauce.

SERVES
8

coffee meringues

2 large egg whites

6 tablespoons granulated sugar

⅓ cup confectioners' sugar

1 teaspoon instant espresso or coffee granules

TO MAKE THE MERINGUES: Preheat the oven to 200°F. On 2 pieces of parchment paper, trace thirty-two 2-inch circles, 1 inch apart. Place the parchment paper, marked side down, on baking sheets. (Placing them pencil side down will prevent marks on the meringues. You will be able to see the outline of the circles when they are inverted.)

With an electric mixer, whisk the egg whites on medium speed until frothy. Add 1 tablespoon of the granulated sugar, increase to medium-high speed with a stand mixer (high speed with a hand-held mixer), and whip until soft peaks form. Add 3 tablespoons of the granulated sugar and continue to whip until stiff, satiny peaks form. Sift together the remaining 2 tablespoons granulated sugar, the confectioners' sugar, and instant espresso or coffee. Fold the dry ingredients into the egg whites.

Place a ¼-inch plain pastry tip in a pastry bag and fill the pastry bag with the meringue (see page 30 for pastry bag tips). Starting from the inside of each circle, pipe the meringue in a solid spiral, filling the circle. Pipe the remaining circles in the same manner. (If you don't want to use a pastry bag, you can carefully spread the meringue into circles with a small offset spatula or the back of a spoon. Use a scant tablespoon for each.)

Bake the meringues until dry, about 5 hours, though you can leave them in the oven overnight. To test if they are done, remove the pan from the oven and let sit on the counter for 30 seconds. Try to remove a meringue from the baking sheet. If it peels off the parchment paper easily, the meringues are done. Let cool for 15 minutes and then put in an airtight container until you are ready to assemble the sandwiches.

continued

coconut ice cream

¾ cup coconut cream, such as
  Coco Lopez

1⅓ cups unsweetened coconut milk

2 cups heavy (whipping) cream

2 tablespoons granulated sugar

⅛ teaspoon kosher salt

¼ cup unsweetened shredded
  coconut, toasted (see page 16)

Cocoa Sauce, warmed (page
  196), optional

flavor twist

· · · · · · · · · · · ·

mexican chocolate ice cream (PAGE 125)
OR
penuche swirl ice cream (PAGE 96)

TO MAKE THE ICE CREAM: Whisk the coconut cream in a medium bowl until smooth. Whisk in the coconut milk, cream, sugar, and salt. Refrigerate for at least 2 hours or up to overnight. Put the coconut in a bowl and put the bowl in the freezer. Churn the ice cream base in an ice cream machine according to the manufacturer's instructions. Fold the ice cream into the toasted coconut. Freeze until scoopable, about 4 hours, depending on your freezer.

TO ASSEMBLE THE SANDWICHES: Turn half of the meringues bottom side up. Place a scoop of ice cream on top. Place a second meringue, bottom side against the ice cream, on top and gently press together to adhere the sandwiches together. (Meringues formed with a spoon or offset spatula are more delicate than piped meringues.) Freeze for at least 1 hour before eating. Serve 2 sandwiches per person. If desired, serve with cocoa sauce.

IN ADVANCE: The meringues can be made up to 3 days in advance as long as the weather is not too humid. I often store meringues in a turned-off oven. Otherwise, they should be stored in an airtight container. The ice cream can be made 2 days in advance. The sandwiches can be assembled 2 days in advance. Store well wrapped in plastic wrap.

biscotti ice cream bonbons

My husband's family goes nuts over my biscotti. Loaded with almonds and full of citrus zest, these cookies often cause a free-for-all when I stack them up on a plate and place them on the table. I have even resorted to giving my father-in-law, Larry, a plastic bag full of them so he can hide them and nibble on them at his leisure. After serving biscotti for years with ice cream, I thought: why not put them *in* the ice cream? This recipe requires a good amount of chocolate for dipping the bonbons, but it is well worth it. I use Vahlrona, as it makes a nice, thin coating of chocolate around the bonbon. If you want, you can substitute chocolate sprinkles, but buy those made by Guittard (see Sources, page 216). They use good chocolate, and they don't taste waxy like other brands do.

MAKES
36
BONBONS

biscotti ice cream

½ cup milk

1½ cups heavy (whipping) cream

⅓ cup sugar

Large pinch of kosher salt

½ teaspoon vanilla extract

1 cup (about 3 ounces) ¼-inch pieces store-bought or homemade biscotti

⅓ cup finely ground biscotti crumbs

18 ounces Vahlrona bittersweet chocolate, chopped

flavor twist

coffee sherbet (PAGE 138)
OR
hazelnut ice cream (PAGE 122)

TO MAKE THE ICE CREAM: Spray an 8-inch square metal pan with nonstick cooking spray and line the bottom and sides with plastic wrap, making sure to press the plastic into the corners of the pan.

Cook the milk, cream, and sugar in a heavy saucepan over medium heat, stirring occasionally, until almost simmering. Pour into a bowl and stir in the salt and vanilla extract. Cool over an ice bath until room temperature. Refrigerate for at least 4 hours or up to overnight. Put the biscotti pieces in a medium bowl and put the bowl in the freezer. Freeze the ice cream base in an ice cream machine according to the manufacturer's instructions. Fold the ice cream into the biscotti pieces. Spread the ice cream in the prepared pan. Freeze until hard, at least 4 hours, depending on your freezer.

TO ASSEMBLE THE BONBONS: Invert the pan of ice cream onto a cutting board. Remove the pan and carefully peel off the plastic wrap. Make 6 lengthwise, then 6 crosswise cuts to yield 36 squares. If the ice cream has softened, put it in the freezer. (I put the cutting board with the ice cream pieces on it right into the freezer.)

Put the biscotti crumbs in a small bowl. One at a time, put the ice cream pieces in the crumbs. With your hands, gently press the crumbs onto the ice cream to evenly coat it. Be careful not to misshape the ice cream pieces. Place in a single layer on a pan. Refreeze until hard, about 30 minutes, depending on your freezer.

Melt the chocolate in a double boiler over hot water. Let cool to room temperature. One at a time, dip the ice cream pieces into the chocolate with two forks, completely coating them with chocolate. Place on a baking sheet lined with parchment or waxed paper. Freeze until hard, about 30 minutes, depending on your freezer.

IN ADVANCE: The bonbons can be made up to 3 days in advance. Once frozen, layer between parchment or waxed paper and store in an airtight container.

fudge cookie and mint chip
ice cream sandwiches

After I develop recipes, I give them to home cooks to prepare. These kind people are able to tell me if a recipe is written clearly, if it works in their kitchen, and most importantly, if it's worth the calories. This ice cream sandwich was without a doubt all the testers' favorite. They agreed that it was worth it to eat salad or go for a jog to allow them to go back for seconds. The great-tasting mint ice cream gets its flavor from fresh mint infused into the milk and cream rather than an artificial extract. The green hue in most mint ice cream comes from food coloring. I prefer not to use any coloring, allowing the pungent mint flavor to speak for itself, but add it if you are so inclined.

MAKES
····· 10 ·····
SANDWICHES

mint chip ice cream

2¼ cups heavy (whipping) cream

¾ cup milk

¾ cup lightly packed fresh mint leaves

1 cup sugar

4 large egg yolks

⅛ teaspoon kosher salt

8 ounces bittersweet chocolate, chopped

fudge cookies

2 ounces (4 tablespoons) unsalted butter

12 ounces bittersweet chocolate, coarsely chopped

⅓ cup all-purpose flour

¼ teaspoon baking powder

¼ teaspoon kosher salt

3 large eggs

¾ cup sugar

2 teaspoons vanilla extract

TO MAKE THE ICE CREAM: In a medium, heavy saucepan, heat the cream, milk, mint, and ½ cup of the sugar over medium heat, stirring occasionally, until almost simmering. Turn off the heat, cover the pan, and steep the mint in the cream for 15 minutes. In a medium bowl, whisk together the egg yolks, the remaining ½ cup sugar, and the salt. Slowly pour the hot liquid into the eggs, whisking as you pour. Return the mixture to the pan and cook over medium-low heat, stirring constantly with a heat-resistant plastic or wooden spatula, until it reaches 175°F and lightly coats the spatula. Strain the mixture into a clean bowl, discarding the mint. Cool over an ice bath until room temperature. Refrigerate for at least 4 hours or up to overnight.

In a food processor, using on-off pulses, grind the chocolate into small pieces. Put the chocolate in a bowl in the freezer. Churn the ice cream base in an ice cream machine according to the manufacturer's instructions. Place the ice cream in the bowl with the chocolate and fold the two together. Freeze until scoopable, about 4 hours, depending on your freezer.

TO MAKE THE COOKIES: Preheat the oven to 350°F. Line 3 baking sheets with parchment paper. Melt the butter and chocolate together in a double boiler over hot water. Stir to combine. Let cool to room temperature.

Sift together the flour and baking powder. Add the salt. With an electric mixer on high speed, whip the eggs, sugar, and vanilla extract together until thick. By hand, stir in the cooled chocolate mixture. Stir in the flour mixture and let the batter rest for 5 minutes.

continued

Using an ice cream scoop 2¼ inches in diameter for each cookie, scoop the batter onto the prepared pans at least 2 inches apart. There should be at least 20 cookies. Bake for about 10 minutes, or until the tops crack. They will look set and no longer shiny on top. Let cool and then remove them from the pans with a spatula.

TO ASSEMBLE THE SANDWICHES: Place 10 of the cookies, bottom side up, on a baking sheet lined with parchment or waxed paper. Place a scoop of ice cream on top of each cookie. Top with a second cookie and gently press down on the top cookie to adhere the sandwiches together. Serve immediately, or freeze until ready to serve.

IN ADVANCE: The cookies can be made 1 day before you assemble the sandwiches. Store at room temperature wrapped in plastic wrap.

gingersnap lemon
ice cream sandwiches

I first created this dessert for Mickey and Minnie at Disney's Epcot Food and Wine Festival in Orlando, Florida. Nicole Lago, the Farallon restaurant purchasing agent, and I were a human assembly line as we put together over six hundred sandwiches. It was sweltering in the kitchen, and to keep the ice cream from melting, the Epcot purchasing agents loaned us the winter parkas they wear for putting food away in the large walk-in freezers. We assembled the sandwiches in a freezer. We laughed as our fingers got frozen stiff and thought about how it was 85°F outside. I wrapped each in a strip of parchment paper and sealed it with a Farallon sticker, making pickup and devouring simple. Go to your local paper shop and find a festive sticker of your own.

MAKES
· · · · · *12* · · · · ·
SANDWICHES

lemon ice cream
1½ cups whole milk

3 cups heavy (whipping) cream

Zest stripped from 2 lemons

1 cup sugar

6 large egg yolks

¼ teaspoon kosher salt

2 teaspoons freshly squeezed lemon juice

gingersnaps
1 cup all-purpose flour

1 teaspoon baking soda

½ teaspoon ground cinnamon

1 teaspoon ground ginger

⅛ teaspoon ground white pepper

¼ teaspoon ground allspice

¼ teaspoon kosher salt

4 ounces (8 tablespoons) unsalted butter, softened

½ cup granulated sugar

¼ cup firmly packed brown sugar

1 large egg

3 tablespoons molasses

TO MAKE THE ICE CREAM: Combine the milk, cream, lemon zest, and ½ cup of the sugar in a heavy saucepan. Cook, stirring frequently, over medium heat until almost simmering. In a bowl, whisk together the egg yolks, the remaining ½ cup sugar, and the salt. Slowly pour the hot liquid into the egg mixture, whisking as you pour. Return the mixture to the saucepan. Cook, over medium-low heat, stirring constantly with a heat-resistant plastic or a wooden spatula, until the custard reaches 175°F and lightly coats the spatula.

Strain the custard into a clean bowl and cool over an ice bath until room temperature. Stir in the lemon juice. Refrigerate the custard for at least 4 hours or up to overnight. Churn in an ice cream machine according to the manufacturer's instructions. Freeze until scoopable, about 4 hours, depending on your freezer.

TO MAKE THE COOKIES: Sift together the flour, baking soda, cinnamon, ginger, white pepper, and allspice. Stir in the salt.

Beat the butter, ¼ cup of the granulated sugar, and the brown sugar together until smooth. Stir in the egg. Mix in the molasses. Stir in the dry ingredients in 2 additions. Refrigerate the dough until very firm, at least 3 hours.

Divide the dough in half, wrap each half in plastic wrap, and refrigerate the dough for at least 2 hours or up to 4 days. When firm, roll the dough on a lightly sugared work surface into two 9-inch-long logs.

continued

Preheat the oven to 350°F. Line 3 baking pans with parchment paper. Cut the dough into ½-inch-thick slices. There should be at least 24 cookies. Put the remaining ¼ cup granulated sugar in a bowl. Coat the cookies with the sugar. Place the cookies 2½ inches apart on the prepared pans. Bake the cookies until set and no longer wet looking, 10 to 12 minutes. They will be puffy when you take them out of the oven and will sink as they cool.

TO ASSEMBLE THE SANDWICHES: Place 12 of the cookies, bottom side up, on the work surface. Place a large scoop of ice cream on each. Top with a second cookie, bottom side against the ice cream, and gently press to adhere the sandwiches together. Serve immediately, or freeze until ready to serve. Once frozen, wrap well in plastic wrap or store in an airtight container.

IN ADVANCE: The cookie dough can be rolled up to a week in advance and refrigerated. The sandwiches can be assembled a couple of days in advance.

milk chocolate–chocolate chip **frozen yogurt sticks**

Excluding my chocoholic sister, who keeps several kinds of chocolate near her at all times, many people find chocolate ice cream a bit heavy on a hot summer day. Copious amounts of chocolate may make a delicious, rich ice cream, but it isn't always refreshing. This recipe is the best of both worlds. Using milk chocolate and yogurt decreases the richness, and adding chocolate chips and the chocolate coating keeps my sister happy. The chocolate coating is a variation of Gaston Lenôtre's. Vahlrona chocolate melts thinner than other brands.

MAKES

8

FROZEN POPS

frozen yogurt sticks
⅓ **cup milk**

1¼ **cups heavy (whipping) cream**

6 **ounces milk chocolate, chopped**

2 **cups plain yogurt**

Large pinch of kosher salt

3 **tablespoons sugar**

3 **ounces bittersweet chocolate, finely chopped**

chocolate coating
8 **ounces Vahlrona bittersweet chocolate, finely chopped**

4½ **teaspoons canola oil**

TO MAKE THE YOGURT STICKS: In a medium saucepan, heat the milk and cream, stirring occasionally, over medium heat until almost simmering. Turn off the heat, add the milk chocolate, and whisk until smooth. Transfer the chocolate milk to a bowl and whisk in the yogurt, salt, and sugar. Let cool to room temperature and refrigerate until cold, about 2 hours.

Churn in an ice cream machine according to the manufacturer's instructions. While the yogurt is freezing in the machine, put the chocolate pieces in a bowl and put the bowl in the freezer. Fold the yogurt and chocolate pieces together. Place the frozen yogurt in a pastry bag (you do not need a pastry tip; see pages 24, 30, 31 on how to fill a pastry bag). Pipe the frozen yogurt into the molds. Place a stick in each and freeze until hard, 6 hours to overnight, depending on your freezer.

Unmold the yogurt sticks by running the molds briefly under hot water and then gently pulling on the sticks. Lay the yogurt sticks in a single layer on parchment-lined baking sheets. Freeze until hard, anywhere from 10 minutes to 1 hour, depending on how soft they were when you unmolded them.

TO MAKE THE COATING: Combine the chocolate and canola oil in a double boiler. Fill the bottom part of the double boiler about one-fourth full of water. Heat the water, over medium heat, until bubbles start to appear. Turn off the heat and place the chocolate over the hot water. Stir until smooth. (The chocolate should not get hot; it should barely be warm.) As soon as the chocolate is smooth, pour it into a tall glass that is wide enough to dip the yogurt sticks in. Dip each stick halfway into the chocolate, then lay it on a parchment-lined baking sheet. Freeze until hard, about 30 minutes.

IN ADVANCE: The yogurt sticks can be made up to 2 days in advance. They can be dipped 1 day ahead. Once the chocolate coating has set, place them on a parchment-lined baking pan so they are not touching. Wrap the pan in plastic wrap.

milk chocolate wafer and **chai ice cream dots**

Chai drinks began as a fad but have quickly become a mainstay in American food culture. Made popular by coffeehouses serving variations of chai lattes, chai can now be found on dessert menus across the country. Often, you see or hear the phrase "chai tea," which is redundant, since *chai* is the Indian word for tea. Chai is black tea prepared with spices, such as green cardamom, ginger, cinnamon, and cloves. It has an intriguing balance of flavors that is both sophisticated and comforting; it pairs well with the smoothness of milk chocolate. These delicate sandwiches capture that flavor and are so tiny you can pop one in your mouth in one bite.

MAKES
..... *36* .....
MINI SANDWICHES

chai ice cream
5 green cardamom pods

1 cup whole milk

2 cups heavy (whipping) cream

⅔ cup sugar

4 whole cloves

2 cinnamon sticks

1½ tablespoons black tea leaves

1½-inch piece fresh ginger, cut into 4 pieces

3 large egg yolks

⅛ teaspoon kosher salt

milk chocolate wafers
4 ounces milk chocolate, finely chopped

TO MAKE THE ICE CREAM: Preheat the oven to 325°F. Place the cardamom pods on a baking pan and crush them with the side of a knife. Toast in the oven for 5 minutes. In a medium, heavy saucepan, combine the milk, cream, ⅓ cup of the sugar, the cardamom, cloves, cinnamon sticks, tea, and ginger. Cook over medium heat, stirring occasionally, until almost simmering. Turn off the heat and cover the pan. Let the spices and tea steep for 10 minutes.

In a medium bowl, whisk together the egg yolks, the remaining ⅓ cup sugar, and the salt. Slowly pour the hot liquid into the egg mixture, whisking as you pour. Return the liquid to the pan and cook, over medium-low heat, stirring constantly with a heat-resistant plastic or wooden spatula, until the liquid reaches 175°F and lightly coats the spatula. Strain through a fine-mesh sieve into a bowl, discard the spices and tea, and cool over an ice bath until room temperature. Refrigerate for at least 4 hours or up to overnight. Churn in an ice cream machine according to the manufacturer's instructions. Freeze until scoopable, about 4 hours, depending on your freezer.

TO MAKE THE WAFERS: Melt the chocolate in a double boiler over hot water. Remove from the heat and stir until smooth. Place scant ¼ teaspoonfuls of melted chocolate about 2 inches apart on 2 parchment-lined baking sheets. As you go, use the back of the spoon in a circular motion to spread the chocolate into 1-inch circles. There will be extra circles in case they break. You will need 72 circles. Let the chocolate sit at room temperature until hard, at least 1 hour. (If your kitchen is very hot, place the pan in the refrigerator briefly.) Carefully remove the circles from the baking pan with an offset spatula.

continued

TO ASSEMBLE THE SANDWICHES: Place half of the chocolate circles, bottom side up, in a single layer on parchment or wax paper–lined baking sheets. Using a very small scoop, about 1 inch in diameter (or a melon baller), place a scoop of slightly softened ice cream on top. (If the ice cream is too hard, the chocolate circles will crack.) Cover with a second circle and very gently press down to adhere the circles together. Serve immediately, or freeze until ready to serve.

IN ADVANCE: The sandwiches can be assembled 2 days in advance. Wrap well in plastic wrap and store in the freezer.

ranger cookie and peanut butter ice cream sandwiches

MAKES

• • • • 12 • • • •

SANDWICHES

In this recipe (unlike the chocolate–peanut butter sauce on page 202), you don't need to use natural peanut butter. In fact, Skippy, Jif, and Peter Pan work better, as they are emulsified and create a smoother ice cream. These brands are sweeter than natural peanut butter, but I have compensated for that in the recipe. Steeping the peanuts in the liquid gives the ice cream a richer, nuttier flavor. Ranger cookies are a weekly staple at the staff meal at Farallon. This cookie recipe was brought to the pastry department by Parke Ulrich, Farallon's executive chef.

peanut butter ice cream

2 cups heavy (whipping) cream

2 cups milk

¾ cup granulated sugar

1 cup unsalted roasted peanuts

6 large egg yolks

⅛ teaspoon kosher salt

⅓ cup creamy peanut butter

flavor twist

chocolate–chocolate chunk ice cream (PAGE 183)
OR
penuche swirl ice cream (PAGE 96)

TO MAKE THE ICE CREAM: Heat the cream, milk, ½ cup of the sugar, and the peanuts in a heavy saucepan over medium heat, stirring occasionally, until almost simmering, about 5 minutes. Turn off the heat, cover, and let the peanuts steep in the liquid for 10 minutes. Whisk together the egg yolks, the remaining ¼ cup sugar, and the salt in a bowl. Slowly pour the cream into the egg mixture, whisking as you pour.

Return the mixture to the saucepan. Cook over medium-low heat, stirring constantly with a heat-resistant plastic or wooden spatula, until the custard reaches 175°F and lightly coats the spatula.

Strain the custard into a clean bowl, discarding the peanuts. Cool over an ice bath until room temperature. Whisk in the peanut butter. Refrigerate for 4 hours or up to overnight. Churn in an ice cream machine according to the manufacturer's instructions. Freeze until scoopable, about 4 hours, depending on your freezer.

ranger cookies

4 ounces (8 tablespoons) unsalted butter, softened

½ cup granulated sugar

½ cup firmly packed dark brown sugar

1 teaspoon vanilla extract

1 large egg

1 cup all-purpose flour

½ teaspoon baking soda

⅛ teaspoon baking powder

¼ teaspoon kosher salt

¼ cup unsweetened coconut

½ cup (2 ounces) unsalted roasted peanuts, coarsely chopped

½ cup old-fashioned rolled oats

⅓ cup chocolate chips

TO MAKE THE COOKIES: Preheat the oven to 350°F. Line 3 baking sheets with parchment paper.

In a large bowl, beat together the butter and the granulated and brown sugars until smooth and creamy. Stir in the vanilla extract and the egg. Sift together the flour, baking soda, and baking powder. Add the salt. Stir the dry ingredients into the butter mixture. Stir in the coconut, peanuts, oats, and chocolate chips.

Using about 1½ tablespoonfuls for each cookie, place mounds of the cookie dough 3 inches apart on the prepared pans. Bake until golden brown, about 12 minutes. Let the cookies cool to room temperature before removing them from the pans with a spatula.

TO ASSEMBLE THE SANDWICHES: Place 12 of the cookies upside down. Place a large scoop of ice cream on the cookie. Place a second cookie on top and press gently to adhere the sandwiches together. Serve immediately, or freeze until ready to serve.

IN ADVANCE: The cookie dough can be made up to 3 days in advance. The ice cream sandwiches can be made 2 days in advance. Store in an airtight container.

cinnamon snap rolls
filled with
crème fraîche ice cream

Vanilla is the number-one-selling ice cream, not just because it is everyone's favorite flavor but also because its versatile taste means it can be served with many different desserts. For a change, try crème fraîche ice cream. It goes with everything vanilla goes with, but its slightly tangy flavor gives an added dimension. If your hand gets cold filling the rolls with the ice cream, wear an oven mitt.

MAKES
24
2-INCH ROLLS

crème fraîche ice cream
6 large egg yolks

½ cup sugar

Large pinch of kosher salt

1¼ cups heavy (whipping) cream

¾ cup milk

¼ cup crème fraîche (see page 16)

cinnamon snaps
1½ ounces (3 tablespoons) unsalted butter

2 tablespoons dark corn syrup

2 tablespoons light corn syrup

¼ cup sugar

6 tablespoons all-purpose flour

½ teaspoon Grand Marnier or other orange-flavored liqueur

¼ teaspoon ground cinnamon

TO MAKE THE ICE CREAM: In a bowl, whisk together the egg yolks, ¼ cup of the sugar, and the salt.

Combine the cream, milk, and remaining ¼ cup sugar in a heavy saucepan and cook over medium heat, stirring occasionally, until almost simmering. Slowly pour the cream into the egg mixture, whisking as you pour.

Return the mixture to the saucepan. Cook over medium-low heat, stirring constantly with a heat-resistant plastic or wooden spatula, until the custard reaches 175°F and lightly coats the spatula.

Cool over an ice bath until room temperature. Strain the custard into a clean bowl and whisk in the crème fraîche. Refrigerate for at least 4 hours or up to overnight. Churn in an ice cream machine according to the manufacturer's instructions. Freeze until scoopable, about 4 hours, depending on your freezer.

TO MAKE THE CINNAMON SNAPS: Preheat the oven to 350°F. Line 3 baking sheets with parchment paper.

Melt the butter in a small saucepan over medium-low heat. Add the dark and light corn syrups, the sugar, flour, liqueur, and cinnamon. Stir until combined. Place teaspoonfuls of the batter 4 inches apart onto the prepared pans.

Bake until golden brown, 8 to 10 minutes. Let the cookies cool on the pan for 15 seconds. Using a small offset spatula, remove a cookie and place it upside down on the work surface. Working quickly, roll the cookie around the handle of a wooden spoon. Slip it off the end of the spoon and set aside to cool. Repeat with the other cookies. (If you find the cookies are cooling and becoming brittle faster than you can roll them, return the pan to the oven for 10 seconds to rewarm them.)

continued

flavor twist
· · · · · · · · · · ·

lime ice cream (PAGE 53)
OR
beaumes de venise
ice cream (PAGE 160)

TO ASSEMBLE THE ROLLS: Fit a pastry bag with a ¼-inch plain pastry tip and fill the bag with some of the ice cream. (If the ice cream is very hard, let it soften for 10 minutes in the refrigerator before filling the bag.) Pipe the ice cream into the rolled cookies. Freeze for at least 1 hour or up to overnight. Store in a single layer, wrapped well in plastic wrap or in an airtight container with each layer separated by parchment paper.

IN ADVANCE: The cookies can be made up to 2 days in advance. Store in an airtight container at room temperature. The snaps are best filled with the ice cream the same day they are eaten.

strawberry–passion fruit
popsicles

It is considered rude to look at your seatmate's laptop screen on an airplane. Still, I often got side glances and even bashful inquiries when working on this book during flights. I guess most people's screens show financial spreadsheets and marketing presentations, and it must be refreshing to see someone writing about sweet things. In fact, this recipe grew out of a conversation I had on a flight with a stranger in the window seat next to me. He saw me working on this book, and we got into an entertaining discussion. He said that he occasionally made strawberry pops at home but was ready to try some variations. I offered some flavor options, and this recipe was created.

MAKES
····· 8 ·····
FROZEN POPS

2 pints fresh strawberries
½ cup passion fruit purée (see page 18)
½ cup plus 2 tablespoons water
¾ cup sugar
Large pinch of kosher salt

TO MAKE THE POPS: Hull and halve the strawberries. Purée them in a food processor. Strain the purée through a medium-mesh sieve into a medium bowl, discarding the seeds. There should be about 2½ cups purée. Add the passion fruit purée, water, sugar, and salt to the strawberry purée. Whisk until the sugar is dissolved. Measure the purée and add more water as necessary to make 3⅓ cups purée. Stir until blended.

TO ASSEMBLE THE POPS: Pour the purée into Popsicle molds. Insert sticks and freeze until hard, 6 hours to overnight, depending on your freezer. Unmold the pops by running the molds briefly under hot water and then gently pulling on the sticks. Lay the pops in a single layer on parchment-lined baking sheets. Freeze until hard, anywhere from 10 minutes to 1 hour, depending on how soft they were when you unmolded them.

IN ADVANCE: The Popsicles can be made up to 3 days in advance. Wrap individually in plastic wrap.

shortcake and rum raisin
ice cream sandwiches

The Italians make a to-die-for ice cream sandwich with brioche and gelato. To Americans it's a bit unconventional—rolls and ice cream? But I assure you, it tastes incredible. In this recipe, instead of having to prepare time-consuming brioches, I use a light, buttery biscuit. Now you can try this Italian-inspired treat without getting on an airplane.

MAKES
· · · · · 10 · · · · ·
SANDWICHES

rum raisin ice cream

¼ cup water

¾ cup sugar

2 tablespoons plus ¼ cup dark rum

½ cup raisins

½ cup golden raisins

3 large egg yolks

⅛ teaspoon kosher salt

1 cup milk

2⅓ cups heavy (whipping) cream

½ vanilla bean, halved lengthwise and seeds scraped out

TO MAKE THE ICE CREAM: In a small, heavy saucepan, combine the water, ¼ cup of the sugar, and the 2 tablespoons rum. Cook over medium-low heat, stirring occasionally, until the sugar dissolves, about 2 minutes. (If the rum catches on fire while the liquid is reducing, cover with a lid briefly to extinguish the flame.) Add the raisins and cook until the raisins are soft and most of the liquid is reduced, about 5 minutes. In a large bowl, whisk together the egg yolks, ¼ cup of the sugar, and the salt. Combine the milk, cream, the remaining ¼ cup sugar, and the vanilla bean and seeds in a heavy saucepan. Cook over medium heat, stirring occasionally, until almost simmering. Slowly pour the milk-and-cream mixture into the egg-and-sugar mixture, whisking as you pour.

Return the egg mixture to the saucepan. Cook over medium-low heat, stirring constantly with a heat-resistant plastic or wooden spatula, until the custard reaches 175°F and lightly coats the spatula.

Strain the custard into a clean bowl, discarding the vanilla bean, and cool over an ice bath until room temperature. Put the ¼ cup rum in a small saucepan. Cook over medium heat until reduced by half. (If the rum catches on fire while the liquid is reducing, briefly cover the pan with a lid to extinguish the flame.) Cool to room temperature. Add the reduced rum to the custard and refrigerate for at least 4 hours or up to overnight. Churn in an ice cream machine according to the manufacturer's instructions. Freeze until scoopable, about 4 hours, depending on your freezer.

shortcakes

2 cups all-purpose flour

⅓ cup sugar

1 tablespoon baking powder

⅛ teaspoon kosher salt

3½ ounces (7 tablespoons) cold unsalted butter, cut into ½-inch pieces

2 large eggs

½ cup heavy (whipping) cream

flavor twist

pistachio ice cream (PAGE 37)
OR
blackberry ice cream (PAGE 162)

TO MAKE THE SHORTCAKES: Preheat the oven to 350°F. Line 2 baking sheets with parchment paper. Sift together the flour, sugar, and baking powder into a large bowl or the bowl of a stand mixer. Stir in the salt. Add the butter and, using 2 dinner knives, a pastry blender, or the paddle attachment of the electric mixer on low speed, mix until the butter is pea-sized. In a small bowl, lightly whisk together one of the eggs and the cream. Add it to the dough and mix until the dough comes together. Gently form the dough into a 5-inch disk. Place the dough on a lightly floured work surface and sprinkle the top lightly with flour. Pat the dough 1¼ inches thick. With a 2-inch-diameter biscuit cutter or drinking glass, cut the dough into rounds. Repeat until you have 10 circles. Place the rounds 2 inches apart on the prepared pans. With a fork, lightly beat the remaining egg in a small bowl. Brush the tops of the shortcakes with some of the beaten egg. Bake until lightly golden, about 20 minutes. Let cool to room temperature.

TO SERVE: Cut the shortcakes in half horizontally. Place a large scoop of rum raisin ice cream on the bottom half of each sandwich. Cover with the top half, gently pressing to adhere the sandwiches together. Enjoy immediately.

IN ADVANCE: The shortcakes are best baked and eaten the same day. The sandwiches should be assembled just before serving.

mini meringue baskets
filled with
pomegranate sorbet

I don't use pomegranates much in my desserts, apart from a garnish here and there. I love their taste, but never feel in the mood to wrestle the seeds out of the fruit. It's messy work. Luckily, you can buy pomegranate juice at the supermarket. Its somewhat bitter taste works wonderfully to complement sweeter dishes. This is especially true with sugary meringues, which when frozen become soft and chewy. These one- or two-bite delicacies are great to serve as a warm-up course for dessert.

MAKES
18
1¼-INCH BASKETS

pomegranate sorbet
1 cup sugar

¾ cup water

2 cups pomegranate juice (see page 18)

1 tablespoon freshly squeezed lemon juice

⅛ teaspoon kosher salt

meringue baskets
1 large egg white

⅓ cup sugar

¼ teaspoon cornstarch

flavor twist

apricot sherbet (PAGE 144)
OR
strawberry ice cream (PAGE 99)

TO MAKE THE SORBET: Stir together the sugar and water in a medium saucepot. Cook over medium heat, stirring occasionally, until the sugar is dissolved and the liquid is reduced to ¾ cup. Transfer the sugar syrup to a bowl and stir in the pomegranate juice, lemon juice, and salt. Refrigerate for at least 2 hours. Churn in an ice cream machine according to the manufacturer's instructions. Freeze until scoopable, about 3 hours, depending on your freezer.

TO MAKE THE BASKETS: Draw eighteen 1¼-inch circles at least ½ inch apart on a piece of parchment paper. Turn the parchment paper over and place it on a baking sheet.

Preheat the oven to 300°F. Whip the egg white in the bowl of an electric mixer on medium-high speed until soft peaks form. Add half the sugar in a slowly, steady stream. Whip until very thick and glossy, 2 to 3 minutes with a stand mixer, or about 5 minutes with a handheld mixer. Fold in the remaining sugar and cornstarch.

Place a ¼-inch star tip in a pastry bag and fill the bag with the meringue (see pages 30–31 for piping tips). Pipe each basket by filling the circle with a single coil of meringue. Continue piping around the outside of the circle until you have formed a round basket about 1 inch high. Bake for 20 minutes. Let cool to room temperature and then remove the meringue baskets with a metal spatula.

TO SERVE: Using a very small scoop or melon baller, fill the meringues with the sorbet. Serve immediately, or freeze until ready to serve.

IN ADVANCE: The meringues can be made 2 days in advance if the weather is not humid. (Otherwise, make and freeze them in the same day.) Store in an airtight container at room temperature. The meringues can be filled with the sorbet and frozen 1 day in advance. Store in a single layer in an airtight container or on a baking sheet wrapped in plastic wrap.

ice cream sandwiches

For my Aunt Mardo's eightieth birthday party, I made caramel ice cream to serve with both a double-chocolate layer cake and a strawberry crème fraîche cake. (If you can't have two cakes when you're eighty, when can you have them? And we had to have room for all the candles.) The next day, we had leftover caramel ice cream but no cake, so for lunch I put together these ice cream sandwiches. · · · · The important part of making caramel ice cream is getting the caramel cooked to the proper color. Too light and it won't have enough flavor, too dark and it will taste bitter. It should be a medium amber color. You shouldn't be able to see through to the bottom of the pan, but it should not be dark brown. When I think it is just about ready, I remove the pan from the heat and let the bubbles dissipate so I can see the color more clearly. (You can always put it back on to cook a little more.) It may take you a couple of times to get comfortable with knowing exactly when it is done, but once you figure it out you will be a pro at using caramel to make many different types of desserts.

caramel ice cream

7 large egg yolks

⅛ teaspoon kosher salt

1 cup sugar

¼ cup water

2½ cups heavy (whipping) cream

2 cups milk

TO MAKE THE ICE CREAM: In a bowl, whisk together the egg yolks and salt. In a heavy saucepan, stir together the sugar and water and cook over medium heat, stirring occasionally, until the sugar has dissolved. Increase the heat to high and cook, without stirring, until the sugar is medium amber in color. Remove the pan from the heat. Slowly stir in about ¼ cup of the cream until combined. Be careful, as the cream will sputter as it is added. Slowly stir in the remaining cream about ¼ cup at a time. Stir in the milk. Slowly pour the caramel cream into the eggs, whisking as you pour.

Return the caramel cream mixture to the saucepan. Cook over medium-low heat, stirring constantly with a heat-resistant plastic or wooden spatula, until the custard reaches 175°F and lightly coats the spatula.

Strain into a clean bowl and cool over an ice bath until room temperature. Refrigerate the custard for at least 4 hours or up to overnight. Churn in an ice cream machine according to the manufacturer's instructions. Freeze until scoopable, about 4 hours, depending on your freezer.

walnut cookies

½ cup (2½ ounces) walnuts, toasted (see page 17)

½ cup sugar

4 ounces (8 tablespoons) unsalted butter, softened

1 large egg

1 cup plus 2 tablespoons all-purpose flour

½ teaspoon baking soda

¼ teaspoon kosher salt

flavor twist
. . . .

orange-cardamom
ice cream (PAGE 104)
OR
pumpkin ice cream (PAGE 133)

TO MAKE THE COOKIES: In a food processor, finely grind the walnuts with ¼ cup of the sugar. In a large bowl, beat the remaining ¼ cup sugar with the butter until smooth. Stir in the egg. Sift the flour and baking soda and stir into the butter mixture. Stir in the salt and ground nut mixture. Wrap the dough in plastic wrap. Refrigerate until hard, at least 1 hour. Roll into a log 8 inches long. Wrap again in plastic wrap and refrigerate until hard, at least 2 hours.

Preheat the oven to 350°F. Line 3 baking sheets with parchment paper. Slice the dough about ¼ inch thick. Place the cookies 3 inches apart on the prepared pans. Bake until golden brown, about 10 minutes. Let cool to room temperature on the pans.

TO ASSEMBLE THE SANDWICHES: Invert half of the cookies bottom side up. Place a scoop of caramel ice cream on top with the remaining cookies, bottom side against the ice cream. Place the remaining cookies, bottom side against the ice cream, on top of the ice cream. Press gently to adhere the sandwiches together. Serve immediately, or freeze until ready to serve.

IN ADVANCE: The cookie dough can be made and refrigerated for up to 1 week. The sandwiches can be assembled and frozen for up to 3 days. Wrap individually in plastic wrap.

Making a milk shake is the simplest way to transform ice cream into a new dessert. It's a conundrum how adding milk and a straw can turn ice cream into a totally different experience. Sodas, milk shakes, floats, and other frozen concoctions sipped through a straw are traditionally enjoyed between meals, but I don't know of any law, state or federal, that forbids one from thinking of them as dessert drinks. Serve them after a meal, just as you would a cake or pie. Just provide a straw and a long spoon. Most conventional float and soda recipes stay close to the original intent. While these are delicious, there are other flavor possibilities beyond a scoop of vanilla ice cream and root beer. A little creativity is all that is needed. Have some fresh berries a little on the mushy side? Purée and combine them with some seltzer water, add sugar as needed, and top it off with a couple of scoops of strawberry ice cream for Very Berry Sodas. Create Purple and Yellow Cows by adding Cassis-Berry Sherbet to pineapple juice and seltzer water. Who says shakes have to be vanilla, strawberry, or chocolate? Blend fresh papaya purée with vanilla ice cream, or combine honey and soy milk ice cream for some new combinations.

through a STRAW

iced espresso floats with
white chocolate ice cream
···· 94 ····

apple cider sodas with
penuche swirl ice cream
···· 96 ····

batido de trigo
(puffed wheat shakes)
···· 97 ····

very berry sodas
···· 99 ····

café viennese yogurt milk shakes
···· 101 ····

lemonade-strawberry floats
with mascarpone ice cream
···· 103 ····

cold italian hot chocolate with
orange–cardamom ice cream
104

honey–soy
milk shakes
···· 105 ····

mango spritzers
with lime sherbet
···· 106 ····

tangerine
creamsicle sodas
···· 107 ····

purple and yellow cows
···· 109 ····

papaya milk shakes
···· 111 ····

watermelon
bubble tea
···· 112 ····

iced espresso floats
with white chocolate ice cream

Italians are as crazy for gelato as Americans are for ice cream, and there are many Italian dessert ideas we can import to this country. Affogato—it translates as "drowned"—is one of them. It is a combination of cold espresso and/or alcohol and any flavor of gelato. The gelato is drowned in the liquid. In Italy, it takes many forms; there is no one classic way to serve it. Here, I take the original concept and flood the ice cream even more for a drinkable version.

SERVES
6

white chocolate ice cream
3 large egg yolks

½ cup granulated sugar

⅛ teaspoon kosher salt

1½ cups milk

1⅔ cups heavy (whipping) cream

4 ounces white chocolate, finely chopped

espresso
6 cups cold brewed espresso or strong coffee

7 tablespoons superfine sugar

flavor twist

peppermint ice cream (PAGE 169)
OR
brown sugar ice cream (PAGE 127)

TO MAKE THE ICE CREAM: In a bowl, whisk together the egg yolks, ¼ cup of the sugar, and the salt. Cook the milk, cream, and remaining ¼ cup sugar in a heavy saucepan over medium heat, stirring occasionally, until almost simmering. Slowly pour the milk and cream into the egg-and-sugar mixture, whisking as you pour.

Return the cream mixture to the saucepan. Cook over medium-low heat, stirring constantly with a heat-resistant plastic or wooden spatula, until the custard reaches 175°F and lightly coats the spatula. Whisk in the white chocolate until smooth.

Strain the custard into a clean bowl and cool over an ice bath until room temperature. Refrigerate the custard for at least 4 hours or up to overnight. Churn in an ice cream machine according to the manufacturer's instructions. Freeze until scoopable, about 4 hours, depending on your freezer.

TO SERVE: Mix together the espresso and superfine sugar in a large pitcher. Fill 6 tall glasses two-thirds full of cold espresso. Place a big scoop of white chocolate ice cream in each glass. Serve immediately, with a long spoon and a straw.

IN ADVANCE: The espresso should be made the same day the float is served.

apple cider sodas
with penuche swirl ice cream

Penuche is a fudgy candy made with brown sugar, cream, butter, and often nuts. I thin it to a sauce consistency and layer it in a chocolate tart or serve it warm over ice cream. Here, I partially fold the cold sauce into vanilla ice cream, creating swirls of buttery brown sugar and rich, creamy vanilla. It is similar to caramel but has a deeper flavor. Apple and penuche are natural partners. Each brings out the best in the other. This soda is best made in autumn, when fresh cider is available.

SERVES
6

penuche swirl ice cream

3 ounces (6 tablespoons) unsalted butter

1 cup firmly packed dark brown sugar

½ cup granulated sugar

⅔ cup heavy (whipping) cream

1½ teaspoons vanilla extract

½ cup (2 ounces) pecan pieces, toasted (see page 17)

½ cup (2 ounces) hazelnuts, toasted, skinned, and coarsely chopped (see pages 17–18)

French Vanilla Ice Cream base (page 116)

apple cider soda

3 cups fresh apple cider or apple juice

6 tablespoons granulated sugar, plus more if needed

Large pinch of kosher salt

3 cups cold seltzer water

TO MAKE THE ICE CREAM: Melt the butter in a medium saucepan. Add the brown and granulated sugars and cook over medium heat, stirring occasionally, until combined, about 5 minutes. Whisk in the butter until smooth. Add the cream and continue to cook, stirring occasionally, for 8 minutes. Stir in the vanilla extract and nuts. Transfer to a bowl and let cool to room temperature.

Churn the French vanilla ice cream base in an ice cream machine according to the manufacturer's instructions. While the ice cream is freezing, put a medium bowl in the freezer. When the ice cream has finished freezing, remove the bowl from the freezer and put the ice cream in it. Place spoonfuls of penuche over the ice cream. Carefully fold the two together, leaving swirls of penuche visible in the ice cream. Freeze until scoopable, about 4 hours, depending on your freezer.

TO MAKE THE SODA: Stir together the apple cider, the 6 tablespoons sugar, and the salt in a large pitcher until the sugar dissolves. Taste for sweetness, and if necessary, add another tablespoon or two of sugar. Stir in the seltzer water.

TO SERVE: Place several scoops of ice cream into each of 6 tall glasses. Pour the apple cider mixture over the ice cream. Serve immediately, with straws and long spoons.

IN ADVANCE: The apple sodas should be prepared just before serving.

flavor twist

cinnamon ice cream (PAGE 166)
OR
butter crunch ice cream (PAGE 42)

batido de trigo
(puffed wheat shakes)

Once, when I joined other chefs for a benefit dinner and cooking class in Miami, we spent a day exploring Little Havana. One of the highlights was this frozen drink, which we enjoyed at a little place called La Feliz de Rey. It sounds bizarre: puffed wheat in a milk shake? But one of the chefs, Cuban-born Maria Manso, owner of Maria Manso World Cuisine in San Rafael, California, had fond memories of slurping it as a kid. You don't have to be a kid to love it. For a real adult drink, splash a little rum over the top before serving. It's breakfast cereal in a glass.

SERVES
4

2½ cups puffed wheat cereal

4 tablespoons sugar

2 cups ice cubes

1½ cups milk

¼ teaspoon kosher salt

TO ASSEMBLE: Combine all the ingredients in a blender. Process until smooth. Pour into 4 glasses and serve immediately.

IN ADVANCE: Batido de Trigo should be made just before serving.

very berry
sodas

Homemade strawberry ice cream often is icy, but not this one. The trick is to cook the strawberries with sugar to a jamlike consistency. This reduces the moisture in the fruit and allows the sugar to coat the berries. It also increases the berry flavor. This technique can be used with most fruits with a high water content. Check the sweetness of the berries and be careful not to add too much sugar, or you will dilute the berry flavor and make the ice cream too sweet. Also, go easy when you mix the remaining sugar into the ice cream base: if it doesn't taste sweet enough, you can easily stir in a little more. This soda is a berry explosion, with strawberries, raspberries, and blackberries. It's the perfect sweet when you can't resist all the berries in the market. If you can find olallie-berries or boysenberries, use them in place of the blackberries. They are in the same family but are plumper and juicier.

strawberry ice cream

1 pint fresh strawberries, hulled and quartered

6 tablespoons plus ¼ cup sugar

½ teaspoon freshly squeezed lemon juice

Large pinch of kosher salt plus ⅛ teaspoon

2 cups heavy (whipping) cream

1 cup milk

TO MAKE THE ICE CREAM: Put the strawberries, the 6 tablespoons sugar, the lemon juice, and the pinch of salt in a medium, heavy saucepan. Cook over medium heat, stirring frequently, until the strawberries reach a jamlike consistency, 20 to 25 minutes. Let cool to room temperature and refrigerate for 1 hour until cold.

Put the cream, milk, the remaining ¼ cup sugar, and the ⅛ teaspoon salt in a medium, heavy saucepan. Cook over medium heat, stirring occasionally, until the liquid is almost simmering. Cool over an ice bath to room temperature. Refrigerate for 4 hours or up to overnight. Stir in the cooked strawberries. Churn in an ice cream machine according to the manufacturer's instructions. Freeze until scoopable, about 4 hours, depending on your freezer.

continued

raspberry soda

2 pints (4 cups) fresh or 24 ounces thawed no-sugar-added frozen raspberries

1 cup minus 2 tablespoons sugar

½ teaspoon freshly squeezed lemon juice

¼ teaspoon kosher salt

4 cups cold seltzer water

¼ cup fresh blueberries

¼ cup fresh boysenberries, olallieberries, or blackberries

flavor twist

· · · · · · · · · · · · · · ·

almond ice cream (PAGE 152)
OR
orange ice cream (PAGE 61)

TO MAKE THE SODA: Purée the raspberries in a food processor. Strain through a fine-mesh sieve, discarding the seeds. There should be about 2 cups purée. In a large pitcher, mix together the raspberry purée, sugar, lemon juice, and salt. Add the seltzer and stir until combined.

TO SERVE: Place several small scoops of strawberry ice cream and some blueberries and boysenberries in each of 6 glasses. Fill with the raspberry soda. Serve immediately, with long spoons and straws.

IN ADVANCE: The raspberry purée can be prepared and sweetened up to 12 hours before serving. Keep refrigerated. Add the seltzer and ice cream just before serving.

café viennese yogurt
milk shakes

I began my culinary career on the savory side of the kitchen. After a year of working in restaurants in New York City, I traveled to France to learn French cooking at the source. At Gerard Pangaud's restaurant in Saint-Cloud, a Paris suburb on the edge of the Bois de Boulogne, we worked split shifts: 9 in the morning until 3:30 in the afternoon and again from 5 until 11 in the evening. During my midday break, I would go to a nearby small café, rest my tired feet, write postcards home, and sip on a café Viennese. The strong coffee with a healthy whipped cream garnish was just what I needed to replenish my energy for the dinner service. It is too tasty a combination to leave in France, so here is a frozen interpretation.

SERVES
6

coffee frozen yogurt

1¼ cups milk

1 cup heavy (whipping) cream

4 tablespoons ground dark-roast coffee

3¼ cups plain yogurt

¾ cup sugar

⅛ teaspoon kosher salt

¾ cup plain yogurt

⅓ cup milk, plus more if needed

1½ cups Chantilly Cream (page 205)

TO MAKE THE FROZEN YOGURT: Heat the milk, cream, and ground coffee in a medium saucepan over medium heat until hot. Turn off the heat, cover, and steep for 10 minutes.

Put the 3¼ cups yogurt, sugar, and kosher salt in a medium bowl. Strain the cream through a fine-mesh sieve into the yogurt, discarding the coffee. Whisk together until smooth. Refrigerate for at least 2 hours or up to overnight. Churn in an ice cream machine according to the manufacturer's instructions.

TO MAKE THE MILK SHAKES: If the frozen yogurt has just been churned, put it in a bowl and whisk in the ¾ cup yogurt and the ⅓ cup milk. If you have made the frozen yogurt earlier and it is hard, put it in a food processor or blender with the ¾ cup yogurt and the ⅓ cup milk. Process until smooth. Add a little more milk for a thinner shake. Pour into 6 glasses. Top with some Chantilly cream. Serve immediately.

IN ADVANCE: Make the milk shakes just before serving.

lemonade-strawberry floats
with mascarpone ice cream

The kids next door were having a difficult time getting much business at their lemonade stand at the end of the street. It was hot, without a cloud in the sky, perfect weather for selling lemonade, but to their disappointment people honked their car horns and waved but didn't stop. I took over some mascarpone ice cream from my freezer, along with some strawberries and seltzer water, and taught them how to make this float. They sold out in no time.

SERVES
8

mascarpone ice cream
4 large egg yolks

¾ cup sugar

⅛ teaspoon kosher salt

2 cups milk

1½ cups heavy (whipping) cream

½ vanilla bean, halved lengthwise with seeds scraped out, or 2 teaspoons vanilla extract

1 cup mascarpone cheese

1 cup minus 1 tablespoon freshly squeezed lemon juice

1 cup sugar

⅛ teaspoon kosher salt

5 cups cold seltzer water

1½ cups chopped fresh strawberries

flavor twist

crème fraîche ice cream (PAGE 83)
OR
blackberry ice cream (PAGE 162)

TO MAKE THE ICE CREAM: In a bowl, whisk together the egg yolks, ¼ cup of the sugar, and the salt. Cook the milk, cream, vanilla bean (if using), and the remaining ½ cup of sugar in a heavy saucepan over medium heat, stirring occasionally, until almost simmering. Slowly pour the liquid into the egg-and-sugar mixture, whisking as you pour. Return the cream-and-milk mixture to the saucepan. Cook over medium-low heat, stirring constantly with a heat-resistant plastic or wooden spatula, until the custard reaches 175°F and lightly coats the spatula.

Strain the custard into a clean bowl, discarding the vanilla bean, and cool over an ice bath until room temperature. Whisk in the mascarpone. Add the vanilla extract (if using). Refrigerate the custard for at least 4 hours or up to overnight. If necessary, whisk the ice cream base to combine. Churn in an ice cream machine according to the manufacturer's instructions. Freeze until scoopable, about 4 hours, depending on your freezer.

TO SERVE: In a large pitcher, combine the lemon juice, sugar, and salt. Stir until the sugar is dissolved. Stir in the seltzer water. Place some strawberries in the bottom of each of 8 glasses. Fill with the lemon seltzer water. Scoop some mascarpone ice cream into each. Serve immediately, with straws and long spoons.

IN ADVANCE: The lemon juice, sugar, and salt can be mixed together and refrigerated for up to 6 hours in advance. Add the seltzer just before serving.

cold italian hot chocolate
with orange-cardamom ice cream

Italians use cocoa powder, sugar, water, milk, and cornstarch in their hot chocolate. The result is a thick beverage unlike the thin, milky American version, yet much lighter than cream-based hot chocolates. Italian hot chocolate is just as good cold as it is hot. The cocoa powder gives it a slight bitter edge, which can be rounded off by adding more sugar if you prefer, though the bitter bite is a nice contrast to the sweetness of the ice cream.

SERVES
6

orange-cardamom ice cream
5 large egg yolks

¾ cup sugar

¼ teaspoon kosher salt

1 teaspoon ground cardamom

2 cups milk

2½ cups heavy (whipping) cream

Zest stripped from 1 large orange

cold italian hot chocolate
1⅓ cups unsweetened cocoa powder

4½ teaspoons cornstarch

1 cup sugar

2⅔ cups milk

2⅔ cups water

flavor twist

candied ginger ice cream (PAGE 64)
OR
coconut ice cream (PAGE 68)

TO MAKE THE ICE CREAM: In a bowl, whisk together the egg yolks, ¼ cup of the sugar, the salt, and cardamom.

Heat the milk, cream, orange zest, and the remaining ½ cup sugar in a heavy saucepan over medium heat, stirring occasionally, until almost simmering. Slowly pour the milk and cream into the egg mixture, whisking as you pour. Return the egg-and-cream mixture to the saucepan. Cook over medium-low heat, stirring constantly with a heat-resistant plastic or wooden spatula, until the custard reaches 175°F and lightly coats the spatula.

Strain the custard into a clean bowl, discarding the orange zest, and cool over an ice bath until room temperature. Refrigerate the custard for at least 4 hours or up to overnight. Churn in an ice cream machine according to the manufacturer's instructions. Freeze until scoopable, about 4 hours, depending on your freezer.

TO MAKE THE HOT CHOCOLATE: Sift together the cocoa powder, cornstarch, and sugar. Heat the milk and water in a heavy saucepan over medium heat until warm. Whisk in the cocoa mixture. Reduce heat to medium-low and cook, stirring constantly with a heat-resistant plastic or wooden spatula until the liquid coats the back of the spoon, about 5 minutes. Pour the hot chocolate into a bowl. Let cool and then refrigerate until cold.

TO SERVE: Divide the cold hot chocolate among 6 mugs or large coffee cups and scoop some orange-cardamom ice cream into each. Serve extra ice cream scoops on the side.

IN ADVANCE: The cold hot chocolate can be made up to 3 days in advance. Keep refrigerated in an airtight container.

honey-soy
milk shakes

Although honey is the primary sweetener here, you still need to add a little granulated sugar for background sweetness and to bring out the flavor of the honey. Using only honey makes the shake taste flat. As is true with fruit, local varieties of honey offer a wider and more diverse selection than what's found in most chain supermarkets. The soy milk will add an earthy element that also brings out the honey's natural flavors.

SERVES
6

honey–soy ice milk
4 cups plain soy milk

½ cup good-quality honey

¼ cup corn syrup

2 tablespoons canola oil

1 tablespoon sugar

⅛ teaspoon kosher salt

1 cup soy milk, plus more if needed

TO MAKE THE ICE MILK: Whisk together the 4 cups soy milk, the honey, corn syrup, canola oil, sugar, and salt. Refrigerate for at least 2 hours or up to overnight. Churn in an ice cream machine according to the manufacturer's instructions. Make the milk shakes now or freeze the ice milk until later.

TO MAKE THE MILK SHAKES: If the soy ice milk has just been churned, place it in a bowl and whisk in the 1 cup soy milk. If you have made the soy milk ice milk earlier and it is hard, put it in a food processor or blender with the 1 cup soy milk. (If using a blender, you may have to purée it in 2 batches.) Process until smooth. In either case, add a little more milk for a thinner shake. Pour into 6 glasses. Serve immediately.

IN ADVANCE: The honey–soy ice milk can be frozen 2 days in advance. Make the milk shakes just before serving.

mango spritzers
with lime sherbet

Fresh mango with fresh lime squeezed over the top is a popular dessert in Mexico and many tropical countries. Simple and refreshing, it's the perfect closure to a meal. Here's a frozen, drinkable version. Serve a small amount for a "first course" dessert or a large one after a meal. The consistency of the mango purée gives the spritzers a thick, rich texture.

SERVES
6

lime sherbet
1⅓ cups sugar

¾ cup water

2 tablespoons light corn syrup

1½ cups freshly squeezed lime juice

Large pinch of kosher salt

½ cup milk

½ cup heavy (whipping) cream

3 large mangoes

6 cups cold seltzer water

6 tablespoons sugar

Large pinch of kosher salt

TO MAKE THE SHERBET: Stir together the sugar, ¼ cup of the water, and the corn syrup in a medium saucepan. Bring to a boil over medium-high heat and cook, stirring occasionally, until the sugar is completely dissolved, about 15 seconds. Remove from the heat and let cool to room temperature. Whisk in the remaining ½ cup water, the lime juice, salt, milk, and cream. Refrigerate until cold, at least 2 hours or up to overnight. Churn in an ice cream machine according to the manufacturer's instructions. Freeze until scoopable, about 4 hours, depending on your freezer.

TO SERVE: Peel the mangoes and remove the flesh from the pit. Purée the mango flesh in a food processor and strain through a medium-mesh sieve. There should be about 2¼ cups purée. Stir together the mango purée, seltzer water, sugar, and salt. Pour the liquid into 6 tall glasses. Add several small scoops of sherbet to each glass. Serve immediately with long spoons and straws.

IN ADVANCE: The mango purée can be made and refrigerated for up to 4 hours. Cover to prevent discoloration. The spritzers should be assembled just before you serve them.

flavor twist

candied ginger ice cream (PAGE 64)
OR
rich vanilla ice cream (PAGE 107)

tangerine
creamsicle sodas

Many people believe vanilla ice cream is a simple flavor to create, but it is actually the most difficult. Vanilla is straightforward and pure. There are no big chunks of chocolate, chopped nuts, or fruit purées to alter the flavor. Vanilla ice cream is ice cream unplugged. The only flavoring is the vanilla, so it is crucial to use the best beans or extract, such as Nielsen-Massey. Here's an old, trusted combination of orange and cream in a new drinkable variation.

SERVES
6

rich vanilla ice cream
8 large egg yolks

1 cup sugar

⅛ teaspoon kosher salt

1 cup milk

3 cups heavy (whipping) cream

4 ounces (8 tablespoons) unsalted butter, cut into 8 pieces

1 teaspoon vanilla extract

tangerine soda
2½ cups cold freshly squeezed tangerine juice

⅛ teaspoon kosher salt

2 teaspoons freshly squeezed lemon juice

6 tablespoons sugar, or more as needed

3 cups cold seltzer water

TO MAKE THE ICE CREAM: In a bowl, whisk together the egg yolks, ½ cup of the sugar, and the salt. Cook the milk, cream, and remaining ½ cup sugar in a heavy saucepan over medium heat, stirring occasionally, until almost simmering. Slowly pour the milk and cream into the egg mixture, whisking as you pour. Return the mixture to the saucepan. Cook over medium-low heat, stirring constantly with a heat-resistant plastic or wooden spatula, until the custard reaches 175°F and lightly coats the spatula. Remove from the heat and strain though a medium-mesh sieve into a clean bowl. Whisk in the butter.

Cool over an ice bath until room temperature. Stir in the vanilla extract. Refrigerate for 4 hours. Churn in an ice cream machine according to the manufacturer's instructions. Freeze until scoopable, about 4 hours, depending on your freezer.

TO MAKE THE SODA: In a large pitcher, stir together the tangerine juice, salt, lemon juice, sugar, and seltzer water. Taste for sweetness and add more sugar if desired.

TO SERVE: Divide the soda among 6 tall glasses. Put 2 or 3 scoops of ice cream in each glass. Serve immediately, with straws and long spoons.

IN ADVANCE: The sodas should be prepared right before serving.

flavor twist

crème fraîche ice cream (PAGE 83)
OR
candied ginger ice cream (PAGE 64)

purple and yellow COWS

The black cow, also known as a root beer float, is simply a catchy name for a classic treat. This purple and yellow cow builds on the original idea but uses pineapple juice and cassis-berry sherbet. The addition of shaved ice makes it very refreshing. It is as good as the original, but has a more vivid presentation and sophisticated taste.

SERVES
8

cassis-berry sherbet

1¾ cups milk

¾ cup heavy (whipping) cream

⅔ cup water

1 cup sugar

⅓ cup light corn syrup

⅛ teaspoon kosher salt

1½ pints (3 cups) fresh blackberries

3 tablespoons crème de cassis

1 teaspoon freshly squeezed lemon juice

TO MAKE THE SHERBET: In a bowl, whisk together the milk, cream, water, sugar, corn syrup, and salt in a medium, heavy saucepan. Cook over medium heat, stirring occasionally, until almost simmering. Transfer the mixture to a bowl and cool over an ice bath until room temperature.

Purée the blackberries in a food processor. Strain the purée through a medium-mesh, then a fine-mesh sieve, discarding the seeds. There should be ¾ cup purée. Stir the purée, cassis, and lemon juice into the cream. Refrigerate for 4 hours, or up to overnight. Churn in an ice cream machine according to the manufacturer's instructions. Freeze the sherbet until scoopable, about 4 hours, depending on your freezer.

continued

pineapple soda

2 small fresh pineapples

**6 tablespoons sugar, plus more
as needed**

Large pinch of kosher salt

3 cups cold seltzer water

2 cups ice cubes

flavor twist

strawberry sorbet (PAGE 173)
OR
coconut ice cream (PAGE 68)

TO MAKE THE SODA: Remove the rind from the pineapples. From the top, cut the pineapples into quarters. Remove and discard the core. Cut the pineapple flesh into 1-inch pieces. Purée in a food processor until smooth. Strain through a medium-mesh sieve, discarding the pulp. There should be about 4 cups purée. Refrigerate the purée for at least 30 minutes or up to 24 hours.

TO SERVE: Put the pineapple purée in a large pitcher. Stir in the 6 tablespoons sugar and the salt. Taste for sweetness, adding a little more sugar if necessary. Stir in the seltzer water. Grind the ice in a food processor until it has the consistency of shaved ice. Divide the ice among eight 12-ounce glasses. Fill with pineapple soda. Put several scoops of cassis-berry sherbet in each glass. Serve immediately, with straws and long spoons.

IN ADVANCE: The pineapple purée can be made a day ahead and refrigerated. Mix it with the seltzer just before serving.

ICE CREAM SHOP
profile

Tropical Dreams

FIVE LOCATIONS ON
THE BIG ISLAND OF HAWAII

FACTORY LOCATION: Kamuela, Hawaii.

RETAIL LOCATIONS: Five on the big island of Hawaii. You can also buy ice cream at the factory.

YEAR OPENED: 1987; the present owners bought it in 2001.

OWNERS: Nancy and John Edney.

HOW THE NAME WAS CHOSEN: It's kind of obvious, isn't it?

NUMBER OF FLAVORS IN REPERTOIRE: 160.

MOST POPULAR FLAVORS: Tahitian vanilla, macadamia nut, Kona coffee.

SIGNATURE FLAVORS: Organic white pineapple sorbet, dragon fruit, litchi, white chocolate–ginger.

AVAILABLE FOR SHIPPING: www.tropicaldreamsicecream.com

THE SCOOP: They use local tropical ingredients in many flavors. The cream comes from big island dairies.

papaya
milk shakes

In Hawaii, milk shakes made with fresh papaya are unparalleled. Bursting with flavor from fruit picked off the tree just outside the kitchen door, they are as fresh as they could possibly be. My sister and I were in Hawaii to celebrate our birthdays, and as we sat under the beach cabana with sand between our toes, watching the waves crash against the shore, we realized getting older wasn't too bad after all.

SERVES
6

4 papayas

French Vanilla Ice Cream (page 116) or Rich Vanilla Ice Cream (page 107)

¼ cup milk, or more if needed

TO MAKE THE MILK SHAKES: Peel and halve the papayas. Scoop out and discard the seeds. Cut the papaya into chunks. Process the papaya in a food processor or blender until smooth. Add the ice cream and the ¼ cup milk and process until smooth. If you like your milk shakes on the thinner side, add a little more milk. Depending on the size of your blender or food processor, you may have to make 2 batches. Mix the batches together in a large pitcher. Pour the milk shakes into glasses and serve immediately.

IN ADVANCE: The papaya can be puréed and refrigerated 3 hours in advance. Cover to prevent discoloration.

watermelon **bubble tea**

Bubble-tea shops are as prolific in Asia as coffee shops are in the United States. In San Francisco, we have several shops in Chinatown and Japantown. Bubble tea is a refreshing cold drink infused with fruit purées, powdered flavorings, tea, water, or milk. Whatever their flavor, they all have marble-sized tapioca pearls that sit at the bottom of the drink, resembling bubbles. The pearls have a slightly chewy consistency, not unlike gummy bears. Another signature trait is the fat straw that accompanies it, large enough for the tapioca pearls to be sipped up. Bubble tea comes in different colors, depending on its flavoring. It is as fun to drink as it is delicious.

SERVES
6

black tapioca pearls

2 cups sugar

9 cups water

¾ cup large black tapioca pearls (see page 19)

4 cups diced watermelon

4 cups ice cubes

TO MAKE THE TAPIOCA PEARLS: In a small saucepan, stir together the sugar and 2 cups of the water. Bring to a boil and cook for 30 seconds. Cool to room temperature. Reserve ¼ cup of the syrup in a small bowl and set both aside.

Bring the remaining 7 cups water to a boil in a large saucepan. Add the tapioca pearls and boil until tender and no longer chewy, 30 to 35 minutes. (Different brands of tapioca pearls may take a little longer to cook.) Drain the tapioca pearls, rinse them well with water, and add to the larger amount of cooled sugar syrup.

TO PREPARE THE WATERMELON: Combine the watermelon pieces and the reserved ¼ cup sugar syrup in a blender. Pulse for 30 seconds. Add the ice and continue to pulse until the mixture is of shaved-ice consistency.

TO SERVE: Put about 2 tablespoons tapioca pearls in the bottom of each of 6 glasses. Pour the watermelon ice over the tapioca pearls. Serve with wide straws (see page 216).

IN ADVANCE: Bubble tea should be served immediately after it is made. The tapioca pearls can be made an hour or two ahead. The tapioca pearls will be too chewy if cold or made the day before. The watermelon can be cut a day ahead.

4

Ice cream and sorbets molded into pans make dramatic desserts. I make them often when company comes over, as they serve a good number of people and can be assembled in advance. I can get the mechanics of the dessert done ahead of time, know that it is ready to serve, and be able to focus on other aspects of the party. Some recipes in this chapter use more than one flavor of ice cream or sorbet, so they take a little more time to prepare. They are not more difficult, but they are twice as delicious. Maple Walnut Ice Cream and Coffee Sherbet Bombe, Brown Sugar Ice Cream Chocolate Roulade, Pumpkin–Caramel Lode Ice Cream Pie, and Frozen Crème Caramels are some of the wide variety of molded desserts that can be created.

Since many of these recipes call for two flavors of ice cream or sorbet, I like to make both bases at the same time. This way, you get all the stove-top cooking done at once. If you have an extra ice cream insert or a rock salt machine or one with a built-in Freon unit, you can churn the ice cream bases one right after the other.

Don't worry if you don't have the exact pan for an ice cream cake as specified in a recipe. Just make sure the size is similar. Lining a pan with plastic wrap makes it easier to unmold once frozen. Spray your pan with nonstick cooking spray (the spray keeps the plastic from slipping) and press the plastic wrap into the corners and along all sides of the pan, leaving 1 inch of plastic wrap over the sides of the pan. To remove an ice cream cake or terrine from its pan, if you have a butane torch, place the mold upside down on a flat plate or cutting board and run the flame quickly over the mold to loosen it. If you do not have a blowtorch, turn the pan over and carefully run hot water on the bottom and sides of the pan. Place the cake and pan upside down on a large plate with the plastic edge showing and gently pull on the plastic wrap until the ice cream comes away from the pan. Remove the pan. Carefully peel off the plastic wrap. If the ice cream is soft, refreeze briefly. Cut ice cream cakes and pies with a hot, dry knife. For each piece, dip a knife in a bowl of hot water, dry it off with a towel, and slice.

in a MOLD

red, white, and blue
ice cream cake

On the morning of the Fourth of July, I put the flag up on the front of the house. I like to make my holiday dessert well ahead of time, leaving me plenty of time to watch parades and fireworks. The Fourth wouldn't be complete without homemade ice cream to celebrate the summer, and cake to honor our nation's birthday. This combination of red berry sorbet, vanilla ice cream, and blueberry sauce helps to create a festive spirit for a holiday spent at the beach or at a backyard barbecue.

SERVES
8—10

french vanilla ice cream
6 large egg yolks

½ cup sugar

⅛ teaspoon kosher salt

1½ cups whole milk

2½ cups heavy (whipping) cream

1 vanilla bean, halved lengthwise and seeds scraped out

orange cake
1 cup all-purpose flour

¾ teaspoon baking powder

¼ teaspoon kosher salt

3 ounces (6 tablespoons) unsalted butter, softened

¾ cup sugar

2 large eggs

1 teaspoon vanilla extract

⅓ cup crème fraîche or sour cream

Grated zest of 1 orange

TO MAKE THE ICE CREAM: In a bowl, whisk together the egg yolks, ¼ cup of the sugar, and the salt. Combine the milk, cream, vanilla bean and seeds, and the remaining ¼ cup sugar in a heavy saucepan. Cook over medium heat, stirring occasionally, until almost simmering. Slowly pour the liquid into the egg mixture, whisking as you pour.

Return the cream mixture to the saucepan. Cook over medium-low heat, stirring constantly with a heat-resistant plastic or wooden spatula, until the custard reaches 175°F and lightly coats the spatula. Strain the custard into a clean bowl, discarding the vanilla bean. Cool over an ice bath until room temperature. Refrigerate for at least 4 hours or up to overnight. Churn in an ice cream machine according to the manufacturer's instructions. Put the ice cream in the freezer.

TO MAKE THE CAKE: While the ice cream is freezing, preheat the oven to 350°F. Grease a 9½-inch springform pan and line the bottom with a round of parchment paper.

Sift together the flour and baking powder. Stir in the salt. In a medium bowl, cream the butter and sugar until light and fluffy. Add the eggs, one at a time, beating until well combined. Stir in the vanilla extract, crème fraîche or sour cream, and orange zest. Add the dry ingredients and mix until combined.

Spread the batter in the pan. Bake for about 20 minutes, or until a skewer inserted in the center comes out clean. Cool the cake completely.

Remove the cake from the pan by running a knife around the inside edge and releasing the latch. Place a cutting board on top of the cake and invert the cake and cutting board together. Remove the bottom of the pan and then carefully remove the parchment paper. Using a serrated knife, cut the cake in half horizontally. Wash and dry the springform pan. Place a cake layer in the bottom of the pan. Spread the vanilla ice cream over the cake. Put the half-assembled cake in the freezer.

red berry sorbet

1 pint fresh or 12 ounces thawed no-sugar-added frozen raspberries

1½ pints fresh strawberries

1 cup sugar, plus more if needed

5 tablespoons water

2½ teaspoons freshly squeezed lemon juice

⅛ teaspoon kosher salt

Blueberry Sauce, warmed (page 193)

flavor twist

cinnamon ice cream (PAGE 166)
AND
plum sorbet (PAGE 181),
OR
butter pecan ice cream (PAGE 40)
AND
blood orange sorbet (PAGE 165)

TO MAKE THE SORBET: Purée the raspberries and strawberries in a food processor. Strain the purée through a fine-mesh sieve into a bowl, discarding the seeds. There should be just under 2 cups purée. Stir the 1 cup sugar, the water, lemon juice, and salt into the purée. Taste for sweetness, adding more sugar as necessary. Refrigerate for at least 2 hours or up to overnight. Churn in an ice cream machine according to the manufacturer's instructions. Spread the sorbet over the vanilla ice cream layer. Place the second cake layer on top of the sorbet, pressing gently to eliminate any air bubbles. Freeze until firm enough to slice, at least 2 hours or overnight, depending on your freezer.

TO SERVE: Unmold the cake by running a small knife around the inside edge of the pan. Release the latch and remove the pan. Cut the cake with a hot, dry knife. Place a slice on each plate and spoon blueberry sauce over the top. Serve immediately.

IN ADVANCE: The cake can be assembled up to 2 days in advance. Wrap well in plastic wrap.

summertime spumoni
with vanilla malt and nectarine ice creams

Spumoni, the classic Italian dessert of layered ice cream and rum-marinated cherries, is mostly ignored these days. Made primarily by large commercial manufacturers, the wonderful nuances of this dessert were lost long ago. These flavors, although not traditional, bring it back to life.

SERVES
10–12

vanilla malt ice cream
¾ cup milk

2 cups heavy (whipping) cream

⅓ cup sugar

6 tablespoons malt powder

cherry-rum cream
Very Cherry Cherries (page 214), cold

¾ cup heavy (whipping) cream

2 tablespoons sugar

1 tablespoon dark rum

TO MAKE THE VANILLA MALT ICE CREAM: In a medium saucepan, combine the milk, cream, and sugar. Cook over medium heat, stirring occasionally, almost simmering. Whisk in the malt powder. Transfer to a bowl and cool over an ice bath until room temperature. Refrigerate for at least 4 hours or up to overnight.

Spray a 6-cup plastic or metal bowl or ice cream mold with nonstick cooking spray and line the bowl with plastic wrap. Place the bowl in the freezer. Churn the vanilla malt in an ice cream machine according to the manufacturer's instructions. Spread the ice cream in the prepared bowl. Freeze until firm, about 1 hour.

TO MAKE THE CHERRY-RUM CREAM: Strain the cherries and coarsely chop them. (Save the liquid for another use.) Combine the cream, sugar, and rum in a bowl and whisk until soft peaks form. Fold in the cherries. Spread the cherry cream over the vanilla malt ice cream. Return to the freezer and freeze until hard, about 3 hours, depending on your freezer.

continued

nectarine ice cream

2½ pounds ripe nectarines

9 tablespoons sugar

Large pinch of kosher salt

½ teaspoon freshly squeezed lemon juice

1⅓ cups heavy (whipping) cream

½ cup milk

flavor twist

mexican chocolate
ice cream (PAGE 125)
AND
orange ice cream (PAGE 61),
OR
lemon ice cream (PAGE 73)
AND
strawberry ice cream (PAGE 99)

TO MAKE THE NECTARINE ICE CREAM: Peel, halve, pit, and coarsely chop the nectarines. Put the nectarines in a medium saucepan with 6 tablespoons of the sugar, the salt, and the lemon juice. Cook over medium heat, stirring frequently, until the nectarines are jamlike in texture, about 15 minutes. Remove from the heat and let cool to room temperature.

Cook the cream, milk, and the remaining 3 tablespoons sugar in a medium saucepan over medium heat, stirring occasionally, until almost simmering. Transfer to a bowl. Cool over an ice bath until room temperature. Stir in the nectarines and refrigerate until cold, at least 4 hours or up to overnight. Churn in an ice cream machine according to the manufacturer's instructions. Spread the ice cream over the cherry cream. Cover with plastic wrap. Freeze until firm enough to slice, 6 hours to overnight, depending on your freezer.

TO UNMOLD AND SERVE THE SPUMONI: Dip the bottom of the bowl in hot water, invert onto a cutting board, and remove the pan. Remove the plastic wrap. If the ice cream has become soft from the hot water, freeze the bombe on the cutting board for 30 minutes. Cut into pieces with a hot, dry knife.

IN ADVANCE: The spumoni can be assembled 2 days in advance. Wrap the unmolded bombe in plastic wrap or aluminum foil.

black mission fig and raspberry **parfaits**

At Farallon, we love to make fig desserts but they don't sell as well as others. Figs make delicious-tasting desserts; there just aren't that many fig-lovers out there. To lure them in, we often combine figs with raspberries, a more popular fruit. People are more willing to give figs a try if they are served with something familiar. Add a frozen compote, and you have something everyone will want to try. They'll be happy they did. Use pasteurized eggs (see page 17) if you are concerned about eating uncooked eggs.

SERVES
6

8 ripe Black Mission figs
1 cup heavy (whipping) cream
⅓ cup sugar
Large pinch of kosher salt
½ teaspoon vanilla extract
3 large egg whites
1 pint (2 cups) fresh raspberries
Berry Sauce (page 192)

TO PREPARE THE PARFAITS: Coarsely chop 6 of the figs. Whip the cream, sugar, salt, and vanilla together until stiff, smooth peaks form. Fold in the chopped figs.

Whip the egg whites until soft peaks form. Gently fold the whites into the cream. Divide the parfait among paper cups, 6 individual ring molds, or ramekins, filling each with ⅔ cup of the mixture. Freeze until hard, about 4 hours, depending on your freezer.

TO SERVE: If you used paper cups, unmold each of the parfaits by cutting a corner of the paper cup and then tearing it from the parfait. Place the parfaits on plates. If you used ring molds, place the parfaits on individual plates, run a small knife around the inside edge of each mold, and remove the molds. If you used ramekins, run a small knife around the inside edge, dip the ramekin quickly in hot water, and invert onto plates, removing the ramekin.

Slice the remaining 2 figs. Place some raspberries and figs on top of and around each parfait. Drizzle some berry sauce over the fruit. Serve immediately.

IN ADVANCE: The parfaits can be made up to 3 days in advance. Once frozen, cover with plastic wrap.

hazelnut, espresso, and chocolate **neapolitan**

A blended combination of hazelnut and chocolate, gianduja is popular in truffles and gelato. Italian in origin, it is one of those ingredients that is universally loved. In this recipe, I layer hazelnut ice cream and chocolate sauce side by side, then add a second layer of ice cream with another Italian favorite, espresso.

SERVES
10

espresso ice cream
4 large egg yolks

6 tablespoons sugar

⅛ teaspoon kosher salt

⅓ cup milk

1¼ cups heavy (whipping) cream

1 tablespoon finely ground or instant espresso

hazelnut ice cream
4 large egg yolks

6 tablespoons sugar

⅛ teaspoon kosher salt

⅓ cup milk

1½ cups heavy (whipping) cream

⅓ cup (1½ ounces) hazelnuts, toasted, skinned, and coarsely chopped (see pages 17–18)

Bittersweet Chocolate Sauce (page 200)

TO MAKE THE ESPRESSO ICE CREAM: In a bowl, whisk together the egg yolks, 3 tablespoons of the sugar, and the salt in a bowl. Combine the milk, cream, espresso, and remaining 3 tablespoons sugar in a heavy saucepan. Cook over medium heat, stirring occasionally, until almost simmering. Slowly pour the milk mixture into the egg mixture, whisking as you pour. Return the mixture to the saucepan. Cook over medium-low heat, stirring constantly with a heat-resistant plastic or wooden spatula, until the custard reaches 175°F and lightly coats the spatula.

Strain the custard through a fine-mesh sieve into a clean bowl. Cool over an ice bath until room temperature. Refrigerate the custard for at least 4 hours or up to overnight. Churn in an ice cream machine according to the manufacturer's instructions.

Spray a 2-quart loaf pan with nonstick spray and line with plastic wrap. Spread the espresso ice cream in the bottom of the prepared pan. Freeze until firm, at least 1 hour, depending on your freezer.

TO MAKE THE HAZELNUT ICE CREAM: In a bowl, whisk together the egg yolks, 3 tablespoons of the sugar, and the salt in a bowl. Combine the milk, cream, hazelnuts, and remaining 3 tablespoons sugar in a heavy saucepan. Cook over medium heat, stirring occasionally, until almost simmering. Turn off the heat, cover the pan, and let the nuts infuse in the milk for 10 minutes. Slowly pour the milk mixture into the egg mixture, whisking as you pour. Return the egg mixture to the saucepan. Cook over medium-low heat, stirring constantly with a heat-resistant plastic or wooden spatula, until the custard reaches 175°F and lightly coats the spatula.

Pour the custard into a clean bowl and cool over an ice bath until room temperature. Refrigerate the custard for at least 4 hours or up to overnight. Strain the custard, discarding the hazelnuts.

flavor twist

strawberry ice cream (PAGE 99)

AND

candied ginger ice cream (PAGE 64),

OR

raspberry sorbet (PAGE 135)

AND

brown sugar ice cream (PAGE 127)

Warm the chocolate sauce in a microwave or in a double boiler over hot water just until spreadable. Spread about two thirds of it evenly over the espresso ice cream. (Reserve the remaining chocolate sauce for serving.) Freeze the ice cream until the sauce is set, about 30 minutes.

Churn the hazelnut ice cream base in an ice cream machine according to the manufacturer's instructions. Spread the ice cream in the pan over the chocolate sauce. Freeze until hard enough to slice, at least 6 hours to overnight, depending on your freezer.

TO UNMOLD AND SERVE: Dip the bottom of the pan in hot water, invert onto a cutting board, and remove the pan. Remove the plastic wrap. If the ice cream has gotten soft from the hot water, freeze the terrine on the cutting board for 30 minutes. Rewarm the remaining chocolate sauce. Slice the terrine. Place a slice on each plate and drizzle some sauce over the top.

IN ADVANCE: The terrine can be prepared and unmolded up to 2 days in advance. Wrap in plastic wrap. Slice the terrine ahead of time or just before serving. Wrap individual slices in parchment or waxed paper until serving.

frozen marjolaine
with almond meringue
and mexican chocolate
ice cream

A classic French marjolaine is made of nut meringues layered with chocolate butter-cream. In this frozen version, I layer ice cream made with Ibarra chocolate and rectangles of almond meringue. This Mexican chocolate comes in disks and is made of sugar, cocoa nibs, cinnamon, and ground almonds. Normally used for making hot chocolate, it has a less chocolaty flavor than American or European hot chocolate and makes a delicious ice cream.

SERVES
8

almond meringues
½ cup (2 ounces) whole natural
    almonds, toasted (see page 17)

¾ cup granulated sugar

⅔ cup confectioners' sugar

4 large egg whites

mexican chocolate ice cream
1¾ cups milk

2½ cups heavy (whipping) cream

2 disks (6½ ounces) Ibarra Mexican
    chocolate, coarsely chopped

Chantilly Cream (page 205)

Nutty Nuts made with sliced almonds
    (page 212)

TO MAKE THE MERINGUES: Preheat the oven to 200°F. Cut parchment paper to fit 2 large baking sheets. Trace 3 rectangles, each 12 inches long and 4 inches wide, on the paper. (Two will fit on one piece of parchment paper; leave at least ½ inch between them.) Place the parchment paper, marked side down, on the baking sheets. (Placing it marked side down will prevent marks on the meringue. You will still be able to see the marks through the paper.)

In a food processor, finely grind the almonds with ¼ cup of the granulated sugar and all of the confectioners' sugar. With an electric mixer, whisk the egg whites on medium-low speed until frothy. Increase to medium-high speed for a stand mixer, high speed with a handheld mixer, and whip until soft peaks form. Add the remaining ½ cup granulated sugar and continue to whip until stiff, glossy peaks form. By hand, fold in the nut mixture. With a small offset spatula, evenly spread the meringue in the 3 rectangles.

Bake the meringues until dry, 5 to 7 hours. To test for doneness, remove the pan from the oven and let sit on the counter for 30 seconds. Slide a metal spatula under one of the meringues. If it comes off of the parchment paper easily, it is done. If it sticks, return it to the oven. It is okay to leave them in the oven overnight.

TO MAKE THE ICE CREAM: Cook the milk and cream in a heavy saucepan, over medium heat, stirring occasionally, until almost simmering. Add the chocolate and whisk until smooth. Strain the custard through a fine-mesh sieve into a clean bowl. Cool over an ice bath until room temperature. Refrigerate the custard for at least 4 hours or overnight. Churn in an ice cream machine according to the manufacturer's instructions. Freeze the ice cream for at least 1 hour until firm but still spreadable.

continued

peach ice cream (PAGE 176)
OR
lemon ice cream (PAGE 73)

TO ASSEMBLE THE MARJOLAINE: If the ice cream has gotten hard, temper it (see page 29). Gently spread the ice cream over 2 of the meringue rectangles. (If you press too hard, the meringue will crack. If this happens, just piece it back together.) Stack the ice cream and meringue layers on top of each other. Place the third rectangle on top. If necessary, trim the edges of the marjolaine to make it neater. Using a large metal spatula, place the marjolaine on a large platter or baking sheet. Freeze until ready to serve.

TO SERVE: Spread half of the Chantilly cream on top of the meringue. Cover with the nuts. Cut into 8 pieces and serve immediately, with extra cream on the side.

IN ADVANCE: The meringues can be made a couple of days in advance if the weather is not humid. The marjolaine can be assembled and frozen up to 2 days. Wrap well in plastic wrap or aluminum foil.

brown sugar ice cream
chocolate roulade

When I was testing recipes for this book, surrounded by desserts around the clock, I had to invent rules to keep from eating myself out of my wardrobe. The primary one was *no pajamas*. I didn't allow myself to eat desserts in the morning before I got dressed. Coffee and an English muffin were fine, but no sweets. This may seem a bit silly to some, but after churning ice cream or assembling an ice cream cake and putting it in the freezer overnight to harden, I woke up curious to see how things came out. I wanted to head straight from the bed to the freezer, stopping only to get a spoon, but if I start the day with ice cream it makes me crave desserts all day. I tossed this rule when it came to this roulade. Later, after several pieces, I justified my pig-out by telling myself that at least there was coffee in the accompanying coffee caramel sauce.

SERVES
8–10

brown sugar ice cream

2 cups heavy (whipping) cream

¾ cup milk

½ cup firmly packed brown sugar

⅛ teaspoon kosher salt

chocolate roulade

2 ounces bittersweet chocolate, coarsely chopped

1½ tablespoons water

6 large eggs, separated

⅔ cup sugar

¼ cup plus 2 tablespoons unsweetened cocoa powder

⅛ teaspoon kosher salt

coffee caramel sauce, warmed (page 204)

TO MAKE THE ICE CREAM: Combine the cream, milk, brown sugar, and salt in a heavy saucepan. Cook over medium heat, stirring occasionally, until almost simmering. Pour the mixture into a bowl and cool over an ice bath to room temperature. Refrigerate the custard for at least 4 hours or up to overnight. Churn in an ice cream machine according to the manufacturer's instructions. Freeze until firm but still spreadable, about 2 hours, depending on your freezer.

TO MAKE THE ROULADE: While the ice cream is freezing, preheat the oven to 350°F. Spray an 11-inch-by-17-inch baking pan with nonstick cooking spray and line the bottom with parchment paper.

Melt the chocolate and water together in a double boiler over hot water. Stir until smooth.

Whip the egg yolks on high speed until light in color, 2 to 3 minutes with a stand mixer, 3 to 4 minutes with a hand mixer. Reduce to medium speed and add ⅓ cup of the sugar. Increase speed to high and continue to whip until thick and ribbony. On low speed or by hand, stir in the ¼ cup cocoa powder and the salt. Stir in the melted chocolate.

In a clean bowl, whip the egg whites on medium speed until foamy and beginning to increase in volume. Gradually whip in the remaining ⅓ cup sugar in a steady stream. Whip until satiny, stiff peaks form. In two additions, fold the whites carefully into the chocolate mixture. Gently and evenly spread the mixture in the prepared pan.

Bake for 25 minutes, or until the top of the cake springs back when pressed with your fingertip and a skewer inserted in the center comes out clean.

continued

flavor twist

cappuccino–chocolate chip
ice cream (PAGE 141)

While the cake is baking, lay a clean thin cotton dish towel on the work surface with a short end toward you. Dust an area of the towel the size of the cake pan with the remaining 2 tablespoons cocoa powder. Remove the cake from the oven and run a small knife around the inside edges of the pan. Place one of the long ends of the cake pan on the right side of the towel and invert the pan and the cake on top of the towel so it falls at the end of the towel closest to you and on top of the cocoaed area. Carefully remove the pan and then the parchment paper. If the cake is not sitting at the end of the towel, fold the towel under itself so it is. From the end closest to you, carefully roll the cake and the towel up together like a jelly roll. Let cool to room temperature, about 1 hour.

TO ASSEMBLE THE ROULADE: If necessary, temper (see page 29) the brown sugar ice cream while the cake is cooling. It should be firm but spreadable. Carefully unroll the cake. (If it splits anywhere, carefully push the broken pieces together.) Gently spread the ice cream over the cake with a thin metal spatula, leaving a ¼-inch border on all sides. Reroll the cake without the towel. Place on a large platter or baking sheet. Cover with plastic wrap. Freeze until firm, about 3 hours, depending on your freezer. Cut into slices and serve with the coffee caramel sauce.

IN ADVANCE: The roulade can be made up to 2 days before you serve it. Wrap well in plastic wrap.

frozen
crème caramels

When I started testing recipes for this book, I froze many of the desserts I have baked over the years to see what would happen. There were many that did not work. An angel food cake got chewy, and the baklava tasted the same as always. But simply putting a crème caramel in the freezer was a winner. The high amount of sugar keeps the caramel soft, and the custard freezes smooth and creamy without the use of an ice cream machine.

SERVES
6

3 large egg yolks

1 large egg

½ plus ⅔ cup sugar

Large pinch of kosher salt

½ vanilla bean, halved lengthwise and seeds scraped out, or 1 teaspoon vanilla extract

¾ cup milk

1⅔ cups heavy (whipping) cream

¼ cup plus 3 tablespoons water

TO MAKE THE CRÈME CARAMELS: Whisk together the egg yolks, egg, the ½ cup sugar, and the salt in a bowl. Combine the vanilla bean and seeds, if using, the milk, and cream in a saucepan. Cook over medium heat until the liquid is almost simmering. Turn off the heat, cover, and let steep for 10 minutes. Slowly pour the milk mixture into the egg mixture, whisking as you pour. Strain through a medium-mesh sieve into a clean bowl, discarding the vanilla bean. Cool over an ice bath until room temperature. Add the vanilla extract, if using. Refrigerate for at least 30 minutes or up to overnight.

Preheat the oven to 300°F. Combine the ⅔ cup sugar and the ¼ cup water in a saucepan. Cook over medium-high heat until the sugar dissolves. Increase to high heat and continue to cook until the sugar has caramelized and is medium amber in color. Remove the pan from the heat and slowly pour in the 3 tablespoons water, stirring until smooth. (The caramel will sputter as the water is added, so add a little at a time and stir carefully.) Pour the caramel into six 4-ounce ramekins so it evenly coats the bottom. If necessary, pick up each ramekin and swirl the caramel so it completely covers the bottom. Let the caramel harden for about 15 minutes.

Place the ramekins in a large baking pan. Pour the custard into the caramel-lined ramekins. Fill the baking pan with hot water to come halfway up the sides of the ramekins. Tightly cover the pan with aluminum foil and place the pan in the oven. (Be sure to keep the pan flat as you put it in the oven so the water does not slosh into the ramekins.) Bake until all but the very center of the custards is set, about 50 minutes. Carefully remove the pan from the oven and discard the aluminum foil. Let the custards sit in the pan for 30 minutes or so until they are cool enough to remove from the pan. Place the crème caramels in the freezer and freeze until hard, at least 6 hours to overnight, depending on your freezer.

TO SERVE: Quickly dip the ramekins in a bowl of almost simmering water. Run a knife around the inside edge of each ramekin. Invert the crème caramels on 6 individual plates. Serve as is, or with your favorite fruit.

IN ADVANCE: The custard base can be made a day before you bake the crème caramels. The crème caramels can be made and frozen up to 3 days in advance. Once frozen, wrap in plastic wrap.

ICE CREAM SHOP

profile

Round Top Ice Cream

ROUTE 1
DAMARISCOTTA, MAINE

MOTTO: *Down East Magazine* says "Your sweet tooth can be satisfied with the homegrown taste of Round Top ice cream."

YEAR OPENED: 1924; owned by present proprietors since 1987.

OWNERS: Gary and Brenda Woodcock.

HOW THE NAME WAS CHOSEN: Named after the Battle of Round Top during the Battle of Gettysburg.

NUMBER OF FLAVORS IN REPERTOIRE: About forty-five, most available all the time except for seasonal flavors.

MOST POPULAR FLAVORS: Black raspberry, ginger, vanilla, peppermint.

SIGNATURE FLAVORS: Black raspberry, apple cinnamon, Indian pudding.

WHAT DO THEY DO WHEN IT GETS COLD OUT: They close the retail shop from Columbus Day until April. The ice cream is still available at stores around the area and wholesale.

AVAILABLE FOR SHIPPING: No, you'll have to go to them.

THE SCOOP: In the summer, they make six hundred gallons of ice cream a day. In the winter, they make three hundred gallons a week. Gary's a schoolteacher during the year. Brenda does all the ice cream production herself during the school year.

frozen key lime pie
with crushed sugar cone crust and macadamia nut cream

Key lime pie, popular in Key West and other parts of Florida, is made with the Key lime that grows in that state. The Key lime also grows in California and Texas, where it is known as a Mexican lime. Nowadays, you find Key lime pie listed on menus all over the United States, but real Key limes are seldom used. Key limes are distinctive, about the size of a Ping-Pong ball. They have a thin yellow-green rind, and the juice is less astringent and more fragrant than that of regular limes. If you can't get fresh Key limes, use bottled Key lime juice.

SERVES
8–10

sugar cone crust
12 sugar cones, broken up

3 ounces (6 tablespoons) unsalted butter, melted

key lime curd
6 large egg yolks

2 large eggs

1¼ cups sugar

1 cup Key lime juice (see Sources, page 216)

⅛ teaspoon salt

1 cup heavy (whipping) cream

macadamia nut cream
¾ cup heavy (whipping) cream

1 tablespoon sugar

¼ teaspoon vanilla extract

⅔ cup (3 ounces) macadamia nuts, toasted and coarsely chopped (see page 17)

TO MAKE THE CRUST: Finely grind the sugar cones in a food processor. Place them in a bowl with the butter and stir until combined. Press the crumbs into the bottom and sides of a 9-inch pie pan. Put in the freezer while you make the curd.

TO MAKE THE CURD: In a bowl, whisk together the egg yolks, eggs, and sugar until combined. Whisk in the Key lime juice and salt. Pour into a medium, heavy nonreactive sauce pan. Cook over medium-low heat, stirring constantly with a heat-resistant plastic or wooden spatula until thick, about 8 minutes. The curd is done when you can briefly see the bottom of the pan as you stir it. Cool over an ice bath. Whip the cream until soft peaks form and fold it into the curd. Pour the Key lime cream into the prepared pie shell. Freeze for at least 4 hours until hard.

TO MAKE THE CREAM: In a bowl, whip the cream, sugar, and vanilla extract until firm peaks form. Fold in the macadamia nuts.

TO SERVE: Spread the cream over the top of the pie. Serve immediately.

IN ADVANCE: The pie can be made and frozen up to 2 days ahead. Cover well with plastic wrap. The cream topping can be whipped and refrigerated up to 3 hours ahead. Just before serving, rewhip the cream slightly until firm and fold in the macadamia nuts.

pumpkin–caramel lode
ice cream pie

We never had pumpkin pie for Thanksgiving when I was a kid. Mom and Dad liked chocolate and caramel better. I do appreciate the merits of a good pumpkin pie, but don't feel, as many do, that the November holiday is not complete without it. So here's a Thanksgiving pie guaranteed to keep everyone in my family happy.

SERVES
8

pumpkin ice cream
3 large egg yolks

½ cup sugar

⅛ teaspoon kosher salt

¾ cup milk

1½ cups heavy (whipping) cream

½ teaspoon ground cinnamon

½ teaspoon ground ginger

¾ cup pumpkin purée

chocolate crust
1½ cups chocolate wafer cookie or chocolate graham cracker crumbs

2 ounces (4 tablespoons) unsalted butter, melted

1½ cups cold Classic Caramel Sauce (page 203)

topping
1 cup crème fraîche or sour cream

1 tablespoon sugar

flavor twist

hazelnut ice cream (PAGE 122)

TO MAKE THE ICE CREAM: In a large bowl, whisk together the egg yolks, ¼ cup of the sugar, and the salt.

Cook the milk, cream, the remaining ¼ cup sugar, the cinnamon, and ginger in a saucepan over medium-high heat, stirring occasionally, until almost simmering. Slowly whisk the liquid into the egg mixture. Return the milk mixture to the pan and cook over low heat, stirring constantly with a heat-resistant plastic or wooden spatula, until the custard reaches 175°F and lightly coats the spatula. Strain through a medium-mesh sieve. Cool over an ice bath until room temperature. Stir in the pumpkin purée. Refrigerate for at least 4 hours or up to overnight.

Churn in an ice cream machine according to the manufacturer's instructions. Place the ice cream in the freezer while you prepare the crust.

TO MAKE THE CRUST: In a bowl, stir together the cookie crumbs and melted butter. Press the cookie crumbs into the bottom and sides of a 9-inch pie pan. Freeze for 30 minutes.

Spread the ice cream in the pan on top of the crust. Using your fingers or the end of the handle of a wooden spoon, make about fifteen ½-inch-wide holes in the ice cream. Place the caramel sauce in a pastry bag (you don't need a tip in the bag). Cut the end off the bag. Fill the holes with caramel sauce. (Save any remaining caramel sauce for garnish.) Freeze the pie until hard, anywhere from 4 hours to overnight, depending on your freezer.

TO SERVE: In a bowl, whisk together the crème fraîche or sour cream and sugar. Spread the mixture over the top of the pie. Warm the remaining caramel sauce on the stove top or in a microwave. Serve the pie with caramel sauce in a pitcher on the side.

IN ADVANCE: The pie can be assembled 2 days in advance. Cover with plastic wrap. Top with the crème fraîche just before serving.

lemon-ginger angel food and raspberry sorbet **layer cake**

In a traditional ice cream cake, the ice cream and cake are layered together and then frozen. The emphasis is on the ice cream, and the cake layer is thin. Only the shape and the way it is cut identify it as a cake. Of course, the easy way to enjoy cake and ice cream together is just to plop a hunk of ice cream onto a slice of cake. In the following recipe, the best of both scenarios are combined. The sorbet is first molded in an angel food cake pan so it is the same shape as the angel food cake. Just before serving, it is placed between two layers of cake. If you have two angel food cake pans, you can make the cake and sorbet the same day. If you only have one, make the sorbet the day before you make the cake.

SERVES
8–10
makes one
10-inch cake

raspberry sorbet
2 pints fresh or 24 ounces thawed no-sugar-added frozen raspberries

½ cup sugar

2 tablespoons water

Large pinch of kosher salt

angel food cake
1⅓ cups cake flour

2 teaspoons ground ginger

⅛ teaspoon kosher salt

1¾ cups (about 12) egg whites

1 teaspoon cream of tartar

1¾ cups sugar

Grated zest of 2 large lemons

2 teaspoons freshly squeezed lemon juice

1½ teaspoons vanilla extract

TO MAKE THE SORBET: Purée the raspberries in a food processor or a food mill. Strain the purée through a fine-mesh sieve into a medium bowl, discarding the seeds. There should be about 2 cups purée. In a medium bowl, whisk together the raspberry purée, sugar, water, and salt. Churn in an ice cream machine according to the manufacturer's instructions. Spread the sorbet evenly in a 9½-inch angel food cake pan. Freeze until hard, at least 2 hours, depending on your freezer.

To unmold, run a knife around the inside edge of the tube and around the inside edge of the pan. Pick the pan up by the tube and remove the inner section of the pan. Run a knife between the sorbet and the bottom of the pan. Quickly invert the pan, letting the sorbet fall onto a plastic wrap or parchment-lined unrimmed baking sheet or cutting board. Wrap well and refreeze until you are ready to assemble and serve the cake.

TO MAKE THE CAKE: Preheat the oven to 350°F. Sift together the cake flour and the ground ginger. Add the salt.

In the bowl of an electric mixer, whip the egg whites on low speed until frothy. Add the cream of tartar. Increase speed to medium-high speed for a stand mixer, high with a handheld mixer, and whip until the egg whites are smooth, white, and just beginning to hold their shape. They will still be a bit bubbly and airy. Slowly whip in the sugar and continue to whip until stiff, satiny peaks form.

Transfer the whites to a large bowl. Add the dry ingredients and carefully begin folding them together. When half incorporated, add the lemon zest, lemon juice, and vanilla extract. Continue to fold until completely incorporated.

continued

1 cup heavy (whipping) cream

2 tablespoons sugar

½ teaspoon vanilla extract

½ pint (1 cup) fresh raspberries

flavor twist

blackberry sorbet (PAGE 35)

OR

blood orange sorbet (PAGE 165)

Carefully spread the batter in a 9½-inch angel food cake pan. Tap the cake on the counter to eliminate any air bubbles. Bake until a skewer inserted in the center comes out clean, about 35 minutes. Invert the cake onto its feet and to cool upside down. (If your cake pan does not have feet, invert it onto a glass bottle to keep it from lying directly on the countertop.) Let cool completely.

To unmold, run a knife around the inside edge of the cake pan and around the tube. Hold the tube and pull the cake from the ring. Run a knife between the cake and the bottom of the pan. Carefully pick up the cake and invert it onto a large plate.

TO ASSEMBLE AND SERVE THE CAKE: Combine the cream, sugar, and vanilla in a bowl and whip until soft peaks form. Slice the cake in half horizontally and set the top half aside. Spread about ½ cup of whipped cream over the bottom half of the cake. Slide the sorbet off the baking sheet on top of the cream. Spread ½ cup of cream over the sorbet. Place the second half of the angel food cake on top. Spread the remaining cream on top. Garnish with the fresh raspberries. Slice with a serrated knife and serve immediately.

IN ADVANCE: The cake can be made a day in advance. Wrap the cake in plastic wrap and store at room temperature. The cream can be whipped and refrigerated several hours beforehand. Rewhip as needed just before serving. Assemble the cake just before serving. The texture of angel food cake changes when frozen.

maple walnut ice cream and coffee sherbet **bombe**

I felt a great sense of achievement when I started my friend Susan baking. An investment banker by trade, her personality is perfect for baking—organized and precise—but she never did much of it on her own. Then, some of her work colleagues set up a friendly competition to see who could make the best tarte Tatin. Susan jumped right in, calling me with questions and for reassurance. I told her to relax and have fun. Baking is not just about the finished product. It is about focusing on the task at hand and creating something with your hands. Even if it doesn't turn out quite right, it will still be much better than store bought. Susan has since gone on to have many desserts in her repertoire. This is a recipe we developed together.

SERVES
10–12

maple walnut ice cream

1¼ cups maple syrup

6 large egg yolks

¼ teaspoon kosher salt

2¾ cups heavy (whipping) cream

1½ cups milk

¾ cup (3½ ounces) walnuts, toasted (see page 17)

TO MAKE THE ICE CREAM: In a medium, heavy saucepan, cook the maple syrup over medium-high heat to reduce to ¾ cup. In a medium bowl, whisk together the egg yolks, salt, and reduced maple syrup.

In a heavy saucepan, combine the cream and milk. Cook over medium heat, stirring occasionally, until almost simmering. Slowly pour the cream mixture into the egg mixture, whisking as you pour.

Return the mixture to the saucepan. Cook over medium-low heat, stirring constantly with a heat-resistant plastic or wooden spatula, until the custard reaches 175°F and lightly coats the spatula. Strain through a fine-mesh sieve and let cool over an ice bath to room temperature. Refrigerate for at least 4 hours or up to overnight.

Spray a 6-cup metal or plastic bowl or ice cream mold with nonstick cooking spray. Line it with plastic wrap, pressing it evenly in the bowl and making sure it comes up over the top of the bowl. Place the bowl in the freezer.

Churn the ice cream base in an ice cream machine according to the manufacturer's instructions. While the ice cream is churning, put the walnuts in a medium bowl and place the bowl in the freezer. Fold the ice cream into the walnut pieces. Put the ice cream in the prepared bowl. Cover with plastic wrap (so your hands don't get cold!) and push the ice cream into the bottom and up the sides of the bowl in an even layer, leaving a hollow in the center for the coffee sherbet. (Or, you can press a smaller bowl on top of the ice cream, pushing the ice cream up the sides.) Freeze until firm, about 2 hours, depending on your freezer.

continued

coffee sherbet

1¾ cups milk

¾ cup heavy (whipping) cream

1 cup sugar

⅓ cup corn syrup

1 tablespoon instant espresso or coffee granules

Large pinch of kosher salt

glazed walnuts

¾ cup (3 ounces) walnut halves

7 tablespoons water

7 tablespoons sugar

Classic Caramel Sauce, warmed (page 203)

flavor twist

peppermint ice cream (PAGE 169)
AND
chocolate–chocolate
chunk ice cream (PAGE 183),
OR
pumpkin ice cream (PAGE 133)
AND
maple walnut ice cream (PAGE 137)

TO MAKE THE SHERBET: While the ice cream is freezing, in a medium bowl, combine the milk, cream, sugar, corn syrup, instant espresso or coffee, and salt. Whisk until the sugar and espresso are dissolved. Refrigerate for at least 1 hour until cold.

Churn in an ice cream machine according to the manufacturer's instructions. Spread the coffee sherbet in the bowl on top of the maple walnut ice cream. Freeze until firm enough to slice, at least 6 hours or up to overnight, depending on your freezer.

TO MAKE THE WALNUTS: While the bombe is freezing, combine the walnuts, water, and sugar in a small saucepan. Cook over medium heat, stirring occasionally, until the sugar dissolves. Continue to cook, without stirring, until the sugar begins to turn golden. Pour the nuts and sugar into an oiled baking pan. With a heat-resistant plastic or wooden spatula, scrape any extra caramel from the pan and pour it over the nuts. With a fork, spread the nuts apart so they are right side up and not touching. Let cool until hard, about 30 minutes.

TO SERVE: Dip the bombe in hot water, invert onto a cutting board, and remove the pan. Carefully remove the plastic wrap. If the ice cream has softened from the hot water, freeze the bombe on the cutting board for 30 minutes. Cut into pieces with a hot, dry knife. Place a slice of the bombe on each plate and serve with caramel sauce and the glazed walnuts.

IN ADVANCE: The bombe can be assembled, frozen, and unmolded up to 2 days in advance. The walnuts can be made up to 1 week in advance.

chocolate-covered pecan and milk chocolate **ice cream brownie cake**

My husband always orders chocolate chip whenever we go to an ice cream shop. I don't know how he can get the same flavor over and over without getting bored. For me, it depends on my frame of mind. I don't even have one favorite flavor. If I were forced to rank my preferences, though, this ice cream would be in my top five.

SERVES
10

milk chocolate ice cream

4 ounces bittersweet chocolate, chopped

1¼ cups (6 ounces) pecan halves

5 large egg yolks

¾ cup sugar

¼ teaspoon kosher salt

2 cups milk

2¼ cups heavy (whipping) cream

6 ounces milk chocolate, finely chopped

TO MAKE THE ICE CREAM: Melt the chocolate in a double boiler over hot water. Remove from the heat and stir in the pecans. Spread in a single layer on a parchment-lined baking pan. Let sit at room temperature until hard, about 1 hour. (If the weather is hot, place the chocolate-covered pecans in the freezer or refrigerator to harden.) Coarsely chop the chocolate-covered pecans.

In a bowl, whisk together the egg yolks, ¼ cup of the sugar, and the salt. Cook the milk, cream, and remaining ½ cup sugar in a heavy saucepan over medium heat, stirring occasionally, until almost simmering. Slowly pour the milk and cream into the egg-and-sugar mixture, whisking as you pour. Whisk in the milk chocolate until it is completely melted.

Return the mixture to the saucepan. Cook over medium-low heat, stirring constantly with a heat-resistant plastic or wooden spatula, until the custard reaches 175°F and lightly coats the spatula.

Strain the custard into a clean bowl and cool over an ice bath until room temperature. Refrigerate the custard for at least 4 hours or up to overnight.

continued

brownie layer

4 ounces bittersweet chocolate, chopped

½ ounce unsweetened chocolate

2 ounces (4 tablespoons) unsalted butter

⅓ cup all-purpose flour

¼ teaspoon baking powder

2 large eggs

⅔ cup sugar

1 teaspoon instant coffee

⅛ teaspoon kosher salt

White Chocolate Sauce (page 199)

flavor twist

multi-chocolate ice cream (PAGE 157)

TO MAKE THE BROWNIE: While the ice cream base is chilling, preheat the oven to 350°F. Grease the bottom of a 9-inch springform pan. In a double boiler, melt the chocolates and the butter together. Sift together the flour and baking powder. In a large bowl, whisk together the eggs and sugar. Whisk in the chocolate mixture. Add the sifted dry ingredients, instant coffee, and salt, stirring until combined.

Spread the brownie batter in the prepared pan. Bake the brownie until a skewer inserted in the center comes out almost completely clean, about 15 minutes. Cool completely.

Place the chocolate-covered pecans in a bowl and put the bowl in the freezer. Churn the ice cream base in an ice cream machine according to the manufacturer's instructions. Put the ice cream in the bowl with the chocolate-covered pecans and fold together until the pecans are evenly distributed. Spread the ice cream over the brownie base in the cake pan. Freeze the cake until hard enough to slice, about 6 hours to overnight, depending on your freezer.

TO SERVE: Run a small knife around the inside edge of the springform pan. Release the latch. Place the ice cream cake on a platter. Cut the cake and serve with the white chocolate sauce.

IN ADVANCE: The brownie can be made and the cake assembled 2 days in advance. Wrap in plastic wrap.

s'mores ice cream cake
with cappuccino–chocolate chip ice cream

There's not much you can do to s'mores to improve them. They possess all the characteristics of a great dessert: crunch, goo, and chocolate. Originally made around the campfire, they have become a fixture of our kitchens as well—I guess we just couldn't go camping enough to satisfy our cravings. To make this treat truly over the top, add ice cream. On the East Coast, use Marshmallow Fluff; on the West Coast, use Jet Puff.

SERVES
10

cappuccino–chocolate chip
ice cream

8 large egg yolks

¾ cup sugar

⅛ teaspoon kosher salt

½ cup coffee beans

2 cups whole milk

2½ cups heavy (whipping) cream

6 ounces bittersweet chocolate, chopped medium fine

crust

1¼ cups ground graham crackers

4 ounces (8 tablespoons) unsalted butter, melted

TO MAKE THE ICE CREAM: In a bowl, whisk together the egg yolks, ¼ cup of the sugar, and the salt. Coarsely crush the coffee beans with a rolling pin or the bottom of a saucepan. Combine the milk, cream, the remaining ½ cup sugar, and the coffee beans in a heavy saucepan. Cook over medium heat, stirring occasionally, until almost simmering. Slowly pour the liquid into the egg mixture, whisking as you pour.

Return the cream mixture to the saucepan. Cook over medium-low heat, stirring constantly with a heat-resistant plastic or wooden spatula, until the custard reaches 175°F and lightly coats the spatula. Cool over an ice bath until room temperature. Refrigerate for at least 4 hours or up to overnight.

Place the chopped chocolate in a bowl and put it in the freezer. Strain the ice cream base through a sieve, discarding the coffee beans. Churn in an ice cream machine according to the manufacturer's instructions. Place the ice cream in the bowl with the chocolate and fold together.

TO MAKE THE CRUST: While the ice cream base is freezing, mix together the graham crackers and melted butter. Firmly press the graham crackers in the bottom of a 9½-inch springform pan. Place the pan in the freezer. Spread the ice cream in the prepared pan over the crust. Freeze until firm, about 1 hour, depending on your freezer.

continued

1 cup marshmallow cream

2 tablespoons water

One 10½-ounce package mini
marshmallows

Bittersweet Chocolate Sauce,
warmed (page 200)

flavor twist

peanut butter ice cream (PAGE 80)

In a medium bowl, with a fork, mix together the marshmallow cream and water. Stir in half of the marshmallows. Spread the marshmallow mixture over the ice cream. Sprinkle the remaining marshmallows on top. Freeze until the ice cream is hard, at least 6 hours or up to overnight, depending on your freezer.

TO TOAST THE MARSHMALLOWS: If you have a handheld blowtorch (see page 21), run a knife around the inside edge of the springform pan. Release the latch and remove the ring. Leave the bottom of the pan under the cake. Torch the marshmallows until golden brown.

If you are using the broiler, adjust the rack so the ice cream cake will be 2 to 3 inches from the heating element. Preheat the broiler. Leave the cake in the pan, put it on a baking pan, and place it under the heating element. Broil until golden brown, about 2 minutes. Run a knife around the inside edge of the pan and remove the pan.

TO SERVE: Place the cake on a large plate or platter. Slice with a hot, dry knife and serve with a good amount of the chocolate sauce.

IN ADVANCE: The cake can be made and frozen up to 2 days in advance. Once frozen, wrap it in plastic wrap or aluminum foil. Brown the marshmallows just before serving.

sauternes ice cream and
apricot sherbet cake

Apricots are often invoked when discussing the nuances of wines, especially Sauternes. These silky, sumptuous wines are said to have the aroma, the balance of sweetness, the acidity, and the honeyed creaminess of this fruit. It makes sense that putting them together would create a wonderful dessert. An apricot-vanilla compote tops off this colorful frozen cake.

SERVES
10–12

gingersnap crust

2 cups gingersnap crumbs (page 73, or your favorite store-bought variety)

3 ounces (6 tablespoons) unsalted butter, melted

apricot sherbet

2 pounds fresh apricots, halved and pitted

1 cup granulated sugar

1¾ cups milk

¾ cup heavy (whipping) cream

⅓ cup light corn syrup

Pinch of kosher salt

TO MAKE THE CRUST: In a bowl, stir together the cookie crumbs and melted butter. Evenly press the crumbs into the bottom of a 9½-inch springform pan. Put in the freezer.

TO MAKE THE SHERBET: Put the apricots in a saucepan with ⅔ cup of the sugar. Cook over medium-low heat, stirring often, until the apricots are soft and juicy, about 5 minutes. Remove from the heat and let cool to room temperature. Purée the apricots in a food processor until smooth. Strain the apricots through a medium-mesh sieve, discarding the skins. There should be 2 cups of purée.

Whisk together the milk, cream, corn syrup, pinch of kosher salt, and remaining ⅓ cup sugar in a medium, heavy saucepan. Cook over medium heat, stirring occasionally, until almost simmering. Transfer to a bowl and cool over an ice bath until room temperature. Whisk in the apricot purée. Refrigerate for at least 4 hours or up to overnight.

Churn in an ice cream machine according to the manufacturer's instructions. Spread the sherbet over the frozen crust. Freeze the half-assembled cake until firm, about 1 hour.

sauternes ice cream

3 cups heavy (whipping) cream

1 cup milk

⅔ cup sugar

⅛ teaspoon kosher salt

¾ cup Sauternes wine

garnish

1 pound fresh apricots, quartered and pitted

⅓ cup sugar

½ vanilla bean, halved lengthwise and seeds scraped out

flavor twist

grand marnier ice cream (PAGE 185)
AND
plum sorbet (PAGE 181),
OR
peach ice cream (PAGE 176)
AND
cassis-berry sherbet (PAGE 109)

TO MAKE THE ICE CREAM: Combine the cream, milk, and sugar in a heavy saucepan. Cook over medium-high heat, stirring occasionally, until almost simmering. Transfer to a bowl and cool over an ice bath until room temperature. Stir in the salt and Sauternes. Refrigerate for 4 hours or up to overnight. Churn in an ice cream machine according to the manufacturer's instructions. Spread the ice cream in the pan over the apricot sherbet. Freeze the cake until hard enough to slice, about 6 hours to overnight, depending on your freezer.

TO MAKE THE GARNISH: Put the apricots in a saucepan with the sugar. Add the vanilla bean and seeds to the pot. Cook over medium-low heat, stirring often, until the apricots are soft and juicy, about 5 minutes. Remove from the heat and let cool to room temperature. Discard the vanilla bean.

TO SERVE: Cover the top of the cake with the apricots. Cut with a hot, dry knife. Serve immediately.

IN ADVANCE: The cake can be assembled one day in advance. Cover with plastic wrap. The apricot compote should be prepared the day you plan to serve the cake. For optimal flavor, store at room temperature; do not refrigerate.

chocolate and caramel
ice cream cake

At work and at home, my refrigerator and freezer are always crammed with sweet odds and ends: a cup of caramel sauce, pieces of brownie scraps, a bowl of whipped cream. In the restaurant, we create some of our best staff meal desserts with such tasty bits, but at home I throw them out, often to the accompaniment of anguished cries from family members. With them in mind, I created this out of excess goodies from other recipes. It's turned out to be one of my favorites.

SERVES
6

sugar cone crust

12 sugar cones (5 ounces)

3 ounces (6 tablespoons) unsalted butter, melted

1 cup cold Bittersweet Chocolate Sauce (page 200)

French Vanilla Ice Cream (page 116) or Rich Vanilla Ice Cream (page 107)

1 cup cold Classic Caramel Sauce (page 203)

¾ cup heavy (whipping) cream

2 tablespoons sugar

½ teaspoon vanilla extract

flavor twist

chai ice cream (PAGE 77)
OR
pistachio ice cream (PAGE 37)

TO MAKE THE CRUST: Finely grind the sugar cones in a food processor. Place them in a bowl with the butter and stir until combined. Press the crumbs into the bottom of a 9½-inch springform pan. Freeze for 30 minutes.

TO ASSEMBLE THE CAKE: Briefly heat the chocolate sauce in a microwave or double boiler over hot water just until spreadable. Spread the chocolate sauce in the bottom of the crust. Freeze until set, about 15 minutes. Spread the vanilla ice cream over the top. Again, freeze to set, about 30 minutes. Briefly heat the caramel sauce in a microwave or double boiler over hot water just until spreadable. Spread the caramel sauce over the ice cream. Freeze for another 30 minutes.

In a bowl, combine the cream, sugar, and vanilla extract. Whip the cream until soft peaks form. Spread it over the top of the cake. Freeze the cake until the ice cream and sauces are hard, about 6 hours, depending on your freezer. Cut into slices and serve.

IN ADVANCE: The cake can be assembled up to 2 days in advance. Once frozen, cover with plastic wrap.

tin roof semifreddos
with roasted pears
and spanish peanuts

SERVES
8

fudge chunks

6 ounces bittersweet chocolate, finely chopped

3 ounces (6 tablespoons) unsalted butter, softened

1 teaspoon vanilla extract

¾ cup evaporated skim milk

1½ cups sugar

3 large egg yolks

⅓ cup sugar

¼ cup milk

1 tablespoon orange juice

1⅓ cups heavy (whipping) cream

⅔ cup (3¼ ounces) Spanish peanuts, toasted and skinned (see pages 17–18)

TO MAKE THE FUDGE CHUNKS: Butter a 9-inch cake pan. Combine the chocolate, butter, and vanilla in a medium bowl. In a large saucepan, stir together the evaporated skim milk and sugar. Bring to a boil and cook, stirring slowly but constantly, for about 8 minutes, until a thermometer registers 226°F. Pour the milk over the chocolate mixture. Stir until smooth. Pour into the prepared pan. Press a piece of plastic wrap directly on the surface of the fudge. Refrigerate until firm enough to cut, about 1 hour. Cut one half of the fudge into ½-inch pieces, place on a plate, and put in the freezer to get hard. (Save the remaining fudge for nibbling.)

Fill a medium saucepan one-third full of water and bring it to a low boil over medium-high heat. Whisk together the egg yolks, sugar, milk, and orange juice in a medium stainless-steel bowl. Place the bowl over the pot of just boiling water. Whisk the egg mixture constantly until thick, about 5 minutes. Remove the bowl from the heat and cool over an ice bath, whisking occasionally, until room temperature.

Whip the cream until soft peaks form. Fold the cream, peanuts, and fudge pieces into the egg mixture. Divide the mixture among 8 individual paper cups, ring molds, or ramekins. Freeze until firm, about 6 hours, depending on your freezer.

roasted pears

4 ripe pears

3 tablespoons sugar

3 tablespoons Spanish peanuts, skinned (see page 18)

Bittersweet Chocolate Sauce, warmed (page 200)

TO ROAST THE PEARS: Preheat the oven to 450°F. Peel, halve, and core the pears. Cut the pears into ½-inch pieces and toss them in a bowl with the sugar. Place them in a single layer on a baking pan. Bake until golden brown, 15 to 20 minutes. Cool to room temperature.

TO SERVE THE SEMIFREDDOS: If you used paper cups, unmold each of the semifreddos by cutting a corner of the paper cup and then tearing it from the semifreddo. Place the semifreddos on plates. If you used ring molds, place the semifreddos on individual plates, run a small knife around the inside edge of each mold, and remove the molds. If you used ramekins, run a small knife around the inside edge, dip the ramekin quickly in hot water, and invert onto plates, removing the ramekin.

Place some pears around each semifreddo. Spoon some chocolate sauce over the pears and sprinkle the peanuts over the semifreddos. Serve immediately.

IN ADVANCE: The semifreddos can be made up to 3 days in advance. Once frozen, cover with plastic wrap. The pears can be made a day ahead. Cover the pears and refrigerate but bring to room temperature before serving.

ICE CREAM SHOP
profile

Swensen's

1999 HYDE STREET
SAN FRANCISCO, CALIFORNIA

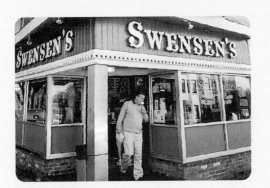

MOTTO: The original slogan in 1948 was "See us freeze."

YEAR OPENED: Founded in 1948 by Earl Swensen; the present owner bought it in 1998.

OWNER: Richard Campana.

HOW THE NAME WAS CHOSEN: Name of first owner.

NUMBER OF FLAVORS IN REPERTOIRE: Forty-five.

MOST POPULAR FLAVORS: Vanilla, Turkish coffee, caramel turtle fudge.

SIGNATURE FLAVORS: Swiss orange chip, thin mint, banana.

WHAT DO THEY DO WHEN IT GETS COLD OUT: Even the fog doesn't affect San Francisco ice cream eaters.

AVAILABLE FOR SHIPPING: No, you will have to visit the shop.

THE SCOOP: This shop has always been independent from the Swensen's Ice Cream chain. They have had some of the same suppliers since 1948.

For many people, dessert isn't complete without a scoop of something frozen. Desserts that include ice cream or sorbet are twice as popular as those without. Yet while crucial, ice cream or sorbet is just one part of the overall taste of a dessert. In Profiteroles with Orange Custard–Chocolate Chip Ice Cream, the crispy light cream puffs and the warm chocolate sauce enhance the flavor of the ice cream. In Warm, Gooey Chocolate Cakes with Chocolate–Chocolate Chunk Ice Cream, the ice cream tastes more intensely chocolaty when served next to the warm cake. With new flavors of ice cream, classic desserts such as apple-pear crisp and crepes are reborn. Combining ice cream with a flaky crust, as in grape tartlets with cinnamon ice cream, or with a light cake, such as plum cake with plum sorbet, makes for contrasting textures that tease the tongue and the palate. The secret when adding a scoop to a dessert is to select a flavor that heightens the essences in the other components and doesn't cover them up. The result is irresistible creations greater than the sum of their parts.

Some care should be taken when adding ice cream to desserts. Pastry chefs often plop it on generously, under the premise that more is better. Ice cream adds richness to a dessert and must be kept in balance with all the other parts of the dish so the dish does not become too intense.

on a
PLATE

almond croquant napoleons
with red wine–roasted strawberries and almond ice cream

When strawberries arrive in the markets in spring, I must use them in my desserts. Their bright red is a delight after the winter and a promise that the weather is changing. Often, early-season strawberries are not as delicious as those that appear later in the season, and they need a little help to enhance their flavor. Slow cooking, assisted by some red wine and sugar, will sweeten early-season strawberries. I often leave them in the oven to cook overnight—the extra time doesn't hurt them, and you wake up to a berry-fragrant kitchen. I should mention that luscious midsummer strawberries at their peak are often too sweet for this dessert and are better eaten plain.

SERVES
6

almond ice cream

1 cup (4½ ounces) whole natural almonds, toasted (see page 17)

3 cups heavy (whipping) cream

1 cup milk

½ cup sugar

Large pinch of kosher salt

red wine–roasted strawberries

3 pints (6 cups) fresh strawberries, hulled

¾ cup Pinot Noir or other dry red wine

3 tablespoons balsamic vinegar

1½ cups granulated sugar

¾ cup light corn syrup

TO MAKE THE ICE CREAM: Coarsely chop the almonds. Heat the cream, milk, sugar, salt, and ¾ cup of the almonds in a saucepan over medium heat, stirring occasionally, until almost simmering. (Reserve the remaining ¼ cup almonds for garnish.) Turn off the heat and cover the pan. Steep the almonds for 15 minutes. Transfer to a bowl. Cool over an ice bath until room temperature. Refrigerate for 4 hours or up to overnight. Strain the milk mixture through a sieve, discarding the almonds. Churn in an ice cream machine according to the manufacturer's instructions. Freeze until scoopable, about 4 hours, depending on your freezer.

TO MAKE THE STRAWBERRIES: Preheat the oven to 200°F. Put the strawberries in a single layer in an ovenproof baking dish. In a bowl, whisk together the wine, balsamic vinegar, and granulated sugar until the sugar is dissolved. Whisk in the corn syrup. Pour the liquid over the berries. Place the pan in the oven and bake until the strawberries shrink and are jammy in texture, about 5 hours.

Strain the strawberry liquid into a heavy saucepan. Bring to a boil over medium heat, reduce the heat to a simmer, and cook to reduce the liquid slightly. Let cool to room temperature and stir it back into the berries. Refrigerate until ready to serve.

almond croquants

¼ cup (1 ounce) sliced almonds, toasted (see page 17)

1 ounce (2 tablespoons) unsalted butter, melted

3 tablespoons firmly packed dark brown sugar

2 tablespoons corn syrup

3 tablespoons all-purpose flour

flavor twist

buttermilk ice cream (PAGE 39)

OR

coconut sherbet (PAGE 173)

TO MAKE THE CROQUANTS: Preheat the oven to 350°F. Line 2 baking sheets with parchment paper. Place the almonds on another piece of parchment paper. Roughly crush them with a rolling pin or the bottom of a small pan. Melt the butter with the brown sugar and corn syrup in a small saucepan over medium heat, stirring occasionally. Remove the pan from the heat and stir in the flour and crushed almonds.

Drop teaspoonfuls of batter about 2½ inches apart on the prepared pans. (The cookies will spread as they bake.) There should be at least 16 cookies. Bake until bubbling and golden brown, 8 to 10 minutes. Let cool to room temperature and then carefully remove from the baking sheet.

TO SERVE: Place a croquant on each of 6 plates. Place a scoop of ice cream on top. Spoon roasted berries and sauce over the ice cream. Top with a second croquant. Serve immediately.

IN ADVANCE: The strawberries can be roasted up to 2 weeks in advance. Cover and refrigerate. The croquants can be made 2 days ahead. Store in an airtight container.

chocolate banana
baked alaskas

Baked Alaska has become one of my family's Christmas desserts, not just for the taste but because everyone loves torching the meringue. Professional pastry chefs use the large propane torches wielded by construction workers, but you can find smaller butane versions at cookware shops. Pyrotechnics aside, this is a classic dessert that has never gone out of favor and can be made in a multitude of variations.

banana ice cream

2 bananas

3 large egg yolks

6 tablespoons sugar

⅛ teaspoon kosher salt

¾ cup milk

1¼ cups heavy (whipping) cream

chocolate cake

6 ounces bittersweet chocolate, finely chopped

4 large eggs, separated

1 teaspoon vanilla extract

1½ tablespoons brewed strong coffee or espresso

Large pinch of kosher salt

⅓ cup sugar

TO MAKE THE ICE CREAM: Preheat the oven to 350°F. Put the unpeeled bananas on a baking sheet. Bake for 10 to 15 minutes, until soft and beginning to give off some liquid. Let cool. Remove the skins from the bananas. Purée the bananas in a food processor.

In a bowl, whisk together the egg yolks, 3 tablespoons of the sugar, and the salt in a bowl. Combine the milk, cream, and remaining 3 tablespoons sugar in a heavy saucepan. Cook over medium heat, stirring occasionally, until almost simmering. Slowly pour the milk and cream into the eggs, whisking as you pour. Return the milk mixture to the saucepan. Cook over medium-low heat, stirring constantly with a heat-resistant plastic or wooden spatula, until the custard reaches 175°F and lightly coats the spatula.

Strain the custard into a clean bowl and cool over an ice bath until room temperature. Stir the banana purée into the custard. Cover and refrigerate the custard for at least 4 hours or up to overnight. Churn in an ice cream machine according to the manufacturer's instructions. Freeze until scoopable, about 4 hours, depending on your freezer.

TO MAKE THE CAKE: Preheat the oven to 350°F. Spray a 9-by-13-inch baking pan with nonstick cooking spray. Line the bottom of the pan with parchment paper.

Melt the chocolate in a double boiler over hot water. In a large bowl, whisk together the egg yolks, vanilla extract, coffee or espresso, and salt until combined. In an electric mixer, whip the whites on medium-high speed until they begin to increase in volume. Whip in the sugar in a slow, steady stream. Continue to whip until stiff, glossy peaks form. Stir the chocolate into the egg mixture. Fold the egg whites into

continued

meringue

½ cup egg whites (about 4)

1 cup sugar

Cocoa Sauce, warmed (page 196)

flavor twist

multi-chocolate ice cream (PAGE 157)

OR

rum raisin ice cream (PAGE 86)

the chocolate mixture in 2 additions. Spread the batter evenly into the pan. Bake until a skewer inserted in the center comes out clean, about 15 minutes. Let cool to room temperature. Run a paring knife around the inside edge of the pan. Place a cutting board on top of the pan and invert the pan and cutting board. Remove the pan and carefully peel off the parchment paper. With a glass or round cutter, cut the cake into eight 2½-inch rounds.

TO MAKE THE MERINGUE AND ASSEMBLE THE BAKED ALASKAS: Place the cake rounds on a baking sheet. Place a scoop of ice cream on each, making sure to leave a little more than a ¼-inch border of cake around the ice cream. Freeze the cakes for 1 hour or up to overnight. If freezing overnight, cover with plastic wrap.

In a bowl, whisk together the egg whites and sugar until combined. Put the bowl in a saucepan of simmering water and whisk constantly until the egg whites are very warm. Remove the whites from the hot water and whip with an electric mixer on medium-high speed with a stand mixer, or high speed with a handheld mixer, until stiff, glossy peaks form and the mixture has cooled to room temperature. Remove the cakes from the freezer. Using a small spatula, spread the meringue over the ice cream, completely covering it but leaving the cake edges exposed. If desired, this can be done several hours in advance. Do not cover. Keep frozen until ready to serve.

There are two ways to bake the Alaskas. You can either brown the meringue with a propane or butane torch (see page 21), or bake them in the oven. If you use a torch, constantly move the flame over the meringue about 1 inch from the surface of the meringue until lightly browned. If you prepare them in the oven, preheat the oven to 500°F. Bake the Alaskas in the center of the oven until lightly browned, about 3 minutes.

TO SERVE: Using a large metal spatula, transfer the Alaskas from the sheet pan onto plates. Serve immediately, with a pitcher of cocoa sauce alongside.

IN ADVANCE: The cake can be made 2 days in advance. Store the cake, well wrapped in plastic wrap, at room temperature, or freeze for up to 1 week. The baked Alaskas can be assembled and frozen for up to 24 hours. Do not cover. Bake the meringue just before serving.

cho cho cho

Julie Ring dreamed up this triple-chocolate creation when she owned Julie's Supper Club in San Francisco. The first cho is a chocolate brownie base, the second a white chocolate ice cream studded with milk and dark chocolate chunks, and the third, a dark velvety chocolate sauce smothering the first two. It quickly became a menu staple. She never considered altering it for fear of an uprising by loyal customers.

SERVES

8

multi-chocolate ice cream

6 large egg yolks

½ cup sugar

⅛ teaspoon kosher salt

1½ cups whole milk

2 cups heavy (whipping) cream

5 ounces white chocolate, finely chopped

4 ounces bittersweet chocolate, chopped into chunks

4 ounces milk chocolate, chopped into chunks

TO MAKE THE ICE CREAM: In a bowl, whisk together the egg yolks, ¼ cup of the sugar, and the salt. Combine the milk, cream, and remaining ¼ cup sugar in a heavy saucepan. Cook over medium heat, stirring occasionally, until almost simmering. Slowly pour the milk and cream into the egg mixture, whisking as you pour. Return the cream mixture to the saucepan. Cook over medium-low heat, stirring constantly with a heat-resistant plastic or wooden spatula, until the custard reaches 175°F and lightly coats the spatula. Whisk in the white chocolate until melted.

Strain the custard into a clean bowl and cool over an ice bath until room temperature. Refrigerate the custard for at least 4 hours or up to overnight. Place the dark and milk chocolates in a bowl and place the bowl in the freezer. Churn the ice cream base in an ice cream machine according to the manufacturer's instructions. Fold the ice cream into the chocolate. Freeze until scoopable, about 4 hours, depending on your freezer.

continued

brownies

8 ounces bittersweet chocolate, finely chopped

1 ounce unsweetened chocolate, finely chopped

5 ounces (10 tablespoons) unsalted butter

3 large eggs

1¼ cups sugar

½ cup all-purpose flour

⅛ teaspoon kosher salt

½ teaspoon baking powder

3 tablespoons unsweetened cocoa powder

Cocoa Sauce, cold (page 196)

flavor twist

espresso ice cream (PAGE 122)
OR
vanilla malt ice cream (PAGE 119)

TO MAKE THE BROWNIES: Preheat the oven to 350°F. Grease the bottom of a 9-by-13-inch baking pan and line it with parchment paper. Melt the chocolates and butter in a double boiler over hot water. In a medium bowl, whisk together the eggs and sugar. Whisk in the melted chocolate mixture. Sift together and then stir in the flour, salt, baking powder, and cocoa powder. Spread the batter in the prepared pan.

Bake until a skewer inserted in the center comes out fudgy and not dry, about 20 minutes. Let cool to room temperature. Run a knife around the inside edge of the pan. Place a cutting board on top of the pan. Invert the pan and board. Remove the pan and carefully peel off the parchment paper.

TO SERVE: Trim the edges off the brownies and cut into 1-by-3-inch rectangles. Place 2 to 3 pieces right side up on each plate. (There will be extra brownies for nibbling.) Place a scoop of ice cream on top of the brownies. Cover with cocoa sauce. Serve immediately.

IN ADVANCE: The brownies can be made up to 2 days in advance. Store at room temperature, wrapped in plastic wrap.

apple-pear crisp
with beaumes de venise ice cream

Apple crisp is a true American dessert. It has been served by cowboys on the open range over a campfire, on farm tables during the Depression, and by suburban housewives in the 1960s. Today, it proudly reigns in American regional restaurants across the country. When gussied up as in this recipe, it even claims a place in upscale dining establishments.

SERVES
8

beaumes de venise ice cream

3½ cups heavy (whipping) cream

1 cup milk

1 cup granulated sugar

¾ cup Beaumes de Venise wine

apple-pear crisp

3 apples, preferably Jonathan, Braeburn, Fuji, or Gala

3 ripe, firm pears, preferably Comice, French Butter, or d'Anjou

⅓ cup granulated sugar

1 tablespoon freshly squeezed lemon juice

Large pinch of kosher salt

About ¼ cup apple juice

¼ cup all-purpose flour

TO MAKE THE ICE CREAM: Heat the cream, milk, and sugar in a saucepan over medium heat, stirring occasionally, until almost simmering. Transfer to a bowl and cool over an ice bath until room temperature. Stir in the Beaumes de Venise. Refrigerate for at least 4 hours, or up to overnight. Churn in an ice cream machine according to the manufacturer's instructions. Freeze until scoopable, about 4 hours, depending on your freezer.

TO MAKE THE CRISP: Peel, halve, and core the apples. Slice them ¼ inch thick. Peel, halve, and core the pears. Slice them ½ inch thick and keep them separate from the apples. Place the apples in a large sauté pan with the sugar, lemon juice, and salt. Cook over medium-high heat, stirring occasionally, for 5 minutes. If the apples don't give off any juice as they cook, add some of the apple juice. Add the pears and continue to cook, stirring occasionally, until all the fruit is soft but still holds its shape. Transfer to a bowl and let cool to room temperature. Stir in the flour and spread the fruit in a 6-cup baking pan.

streusel topping

¾ cup all-purpose flour

⅓ cup firmly packed brown sugar

1 tablespoon granulated sugar

⅛ teaspoon kosher salt

⅛ teaspoon ground cinnamon

⅓ cup (1½ ounces) whole natural almonds, toasted and coarsely chopped (see page 17)

4 ounces (8 tablespoons) cold unsalted butter, cut into 1-inch pieces

flavor twist

butter pecan ice cream (PAGE 40)
OR
rich vanilla ice cream (PAGE 107)

TO MAKE THE TOPPING: Mix together the flour, brown sugar, sugar, salt, cinnamon, and almonds in a bowl. Cut in the butter with a pastry blender or 2 dinner knives until the mixture is crumbly. Refrigerate for at least 30 minutes.

Sprinkle the streusel over the fruit. Bake the crisp in a preheated 375°F oven until the fruit is hot and bubbly and the streusel is golden brown, about 20 minutes. Let cool slightly. Serve warm, with the Beaumes de Venise ice cream.

IN ADVANCE: The fruit and streusel can each be prepared 2 days in advance. Cover and refrigerate. The crisp can be assembled in advance and baked just before serving, or it can be baked several hours in advance and reheated. Store at room temperature.

blackberry ice cream– filled crepes
with orange beurre blanc

One of my favorite things about this recipe is the combination of hot and cold elements. The contrast offers a delicious shock to my taste buds. The hot component intensifies the cold part and vice versa. For a sweet version of beurre blanc, a warm French butter sauce, I use orange juice, which pairs beautifully with the blackberry ice cream.

SERVES
8

blackberry ice cream
2 pints fresh or 24 ounces thawed no-sugar-added frozen blackberries

4 large egg yolks

¼ cup plus ⅓ cup sugar

⅛ teaspoon kosher salt

1 cup milk

1½ cups heavy (whipping) cream

crepes
2 large eggs

⅓ cup water

¾ cup milk

1 cup all-purpose flour

2 tablespoons cornstarch

¼ teaspoon salt

1 ounce (2 tablespoons) unsalted butter, melted, plus about ¼ teaspoon for crepe pan

Grated zest of 1 lemon

½ teaspoon vanilla extract

TO MAKE THE ICE CREAM: Purée the blackberries in a food processor. Strain the purée through a fine-mesh sieve, discarding the seeds. There should be about 1 cup purée.

In a large bowl, whisk together the egg yolks, ¼ cup of the sugar, and the salt. Cook the milk, cream, and the remaining ⅓ cup sugar in a saucepan over medium-high heat, stirring occasionally, until almost simmering. Slowly whisk the liquid into the egg mixture. Return the milk and cream to the pan and cook over low heat, stirring constantly with a heat-resistant plastic or wooden spatula, until it reaches 175°F and lightly coats the spatula. Strain through a sieve into a clean bowl. Cool over an ice bath to room temperature. Stir in the blackberry purée. Refrigerate for at least 4 hours or up to overnight.

Churn in an ice cream machine according to the manufacturer's instructions. Freeze the ice cream until scoopable, about 4 hours, depending on your freezer.

TO MAKE THE CREPES: In a food processor or blender, blend the eggs, water, and milk until combined. Sift together the flour, cornstarch, and salt. Add to the egg mixture and blend. Blend in the melted butter, lemon zest, and vanilla extract. Cover and refrigerate the batter for 30 minutes or up to overnight.

Heat a 6-inch crepe or nonstick pan over medium heat. Lightly grease the bottom of the pan with the ¼ teaspoon butter. Pour about 2 tablespoons of batter into the pan, rotating the pan so that it coats the entire bottom. Cook for 1½ minutes. Using the tip of a knife, loosen a side of the crepe from the pan. With your fingers, flip the crepe over and cook for another 15 seconds. Place the finished crepe on a large plate. Continue cooking crepes, slightly overlapping them on top of each other, to make at least 18 crepes. It is not necessary to grease the pan after making each one. Wrap the crepes in plastic wrap and store at room temperature until ready to use.

orange beurre blanc

2 cups orange juice

1¼ cups sugar

¼ cup heavy (whipping) cream

7 ounces (14 tablespoons)
unsalted butter

Large pinch of kosher salt

1½ tablespoons freshly squeezed
lemon juice

½ pint (1 cup) fresh blackberries

flavor twist

pistachio ice cream (PAGE 37)
OR
dulce de leche
frozen yogurt (PAGE 48)

TO MAKE THE BEURRE BLANC: In a medium saucepan, stir together the orange juice and sugar. Cook over medium heat to reduce to 1 cup. Add the cream and cook for 30 seconds. Reduce to very low heat and whisk in the butter, 1 tablespoon at a time, making sure it is incorporated before adding more. (It is important the sauce does not get too hot, or it will separate.) Stir in the salt and lemon juice. If using soon, keep warm over warm water until ready to serve.

TO SERVE: Place a small scoop of ice cream in the center of each crepe. Fold the crepe into quarters over the ice cream. Place 2 crepes on top of each other, seam side down, on each plate. Spoon some orange beurre blanc over the crepes. Scatter the blackberries around the crepes. Serve immediately.

IN ADVANCE: The crepes can be made 1 day in advance and stored at room temperature. The beurre blanc should be made within a few hours of being served. Keep warm. It can be gently reheated in a double boiler over hot, not boiling water, stirring slowly and constantly, or in a microwave on low heat for 5-second intervals. Do not reheat it too quickly or allow it to get too hot or the sauce will separate.

blood orange–vanilla
creamsicle

The Creamsicle may just be the most famous Popsicle name ever. A well-known fourth-level dressage horse, a rock band from Pennsylvania, a Ralph Lauren bath towel, a variety of corn snake, and a nasturtium are called by the name Creamsicle. San Franciscan Frank Epperson not only conceived of the Creamsicle, he created and patented the Popsicle. Now that is a real claim to fame! This variation uses a spoon rather than a stick, but don't worry, it is just as scrumptious as the original.

SERVES
6

blood orange sorbet

2¾ cups blood orange juice, strained (about 12 blood oranges)

1 cup sugar

2¾ teaspoons freshly squeezed lemon juice

Large pinch of kosher salt

vanilla custard

1 vanilla bean, split lengthwise with seeds scraped out

2½ cups heavy (whipping) cream

1 cup milk

½ cup sugar

2¼ teaspoons plain gelatin

2 tablespoons water

3 blood oranges, peeled and segmented

flavor twist

blackberry sorbet (PAGE 35)
OR
pomegranate sorbet (PAGE 89)

TO MAKE THE SORBET: In a large bowl, combine the blood orange juice, sugar, lemon juice, and salt. Stir until the sugar dissolves. Refrigerate for at least 2 hours or up to overnight. Churn in an ice cream machine according to the manufacturer's instructions. Freeze until scoopable, about 2 hours, depending on your freezer.

TO MAKE THE CUSTARD: Combine the vanilla bean and seeds, cream, milk, and sugar in a medium saucepan. Heat over medium heat, stirring occasionally, until almost simmering. Turn off the heat and cover the pan. Let the vanilla bean steep in the liquid for 10 minutes.

Stir together the gelatin and the water in a small bowl. Let stand for 5 minutes. Strain the cream mixture into a bowl, discarding the vanilla bean. Stir the gelatin mixture into the cream with a heat-resistant plastic or wooden spatula. Let the liquid cool to warm, stirring occasionally, about 10 minutes. (Stirring prevents the gelatin from sinking to the bottom of the hot liquid.) Pour the vanilla custard into 6 ramekins. Refrigerate until set, at least 4 hours.

TO SERVE: Unmold by dipping the bottom of the ramekins in a bowl of very hot water. Run a knife around the inside edge of each cream and invert onto a plate. Arrange the orange segments around the creams. Place a scoop or quenelle (see page 29) of sorbet on top of the vanilla custard. Serve immediately.

IN ADVANCE: The creams may be made up to 2 days ahead. Once firm, cover with plastic wrap.

champagne grape and pecan galettes
with cinnamon ice cream

Grape desserts are rare in the United States but popular in Italy and France, especially during grape harvest. Champagne grapes are a pea-sized variety, traditionally grown just for wine making. Deep purple, they are sweet, seedless, and delicious, whether served with cheese or on a galette such as this. Also known as Cornith grapes, they're grown in Arizona and California and are available in the late summer and fall. If you can't find Champagne grapes, use another flavorful variety such as a Concord. These larger grapes should be cut in quarters and seeded.

SERVES
8

cinnamon ice cream
2¾ cups heavy (whipping) cream

1 cup milk

⅔ cup sugar

2 cinnamon sticks

⅛ teaspoon ground cinnamon

⅛ teaspoon kosher salt

galette dough
1 large egg

5 ounces (10 tablespoons) cold unsalted butter

1¼ cups all-purpose flour

Large pinch of kosher salt

3 tablespoons sugar

TO MAKE THE ICE CREAM: Combine the cream, milk, sugar, cinnamon sticks, ground cinnamon, and salt in a heavy saucepan. Cook over medium heat, stirring occasionally, until almost simmering. Pour the mixture into a bowl and cool over an ice bath to room temperature. Refrigerate for at least 4 hours or up to overnight. Strain the cream, discarding the cinnamon sticks. Churn in an ice cream machine according to the manufacturer's instructions. Freeze until scoopable, about 4 hours, depending on your freezer.

TO MAKE THE GALETTE DOUGH: In a small bowl, whisk the egg until blended. Divide the beaten egg evenly into two small bowls; each will be about 1 tablespoon. Set aside 1 bowl of the beaten egg to use in the pecan filling. Cut the butter into 1-inch pieces. Put it in a medium bowl with the flour, salt, and sugar. With a pastry blender, 2 dinner knives, or an electric mixer fitted with the paddle attachment on low speed, cut in the butter until it is the size of small peas. Add the egg from one of the bowls and stir until a dough forms. Form the dough into a disk about 5 inches in diameter. Wrap in plastic wrap and refrigerate for at least 30 minutes.

pecan filling

½ cup (2 ounces) pecans, toasted (see page 17)

2 tablespoons sugar

1 teaspoon all-purpose flour

1 ounce (2 tablespoons) unsalted butter

1½ cups Champagne grapes

flavor twist

crème fraîche ice cream (PAGE 83)
OR
orange-cardamom
ice cream (PAGE 104)

MEANWHILE, MAKE THE PECAN FILLING: Using on-off pulses, grind the pecans, sugar, and flour in a food processor until medium fine. Add the butter and reserved egg and mix just until combined.

TO ASSEMBLE: On a lightly floured work surface, roll out the dough ⅛ inch thick. Using a small plate or large cutter as a guide, cut into eight 5-inch rounds; reroll scraps of dough as necessary. Fold the outer ½ inch of each round over, pleating as you go, making a 4-inch round. Dock the bottom of the galettes with the tines of a fork. Place on parchment-lined baking sheets and refrigerate for at least 30 minutes.

Preheat the oven to 350°F. Spread 1 tablespoon of the pecan mixture in each galette. Place some grapes over the pecan filling. Bake until golden brown, about 25 minutes. Cool slightly and serve warm, with the cinnamon ice cream.

IN ADVANCE: The galette dough can be made and rolled 1 day ahead. The galettes can be filled several hours before baking. Refrigerate until ready to bake. They should be baked the day they are served. They can be reheated. Store baked galettes at room temperature.

chocolate crepes
with peppermint ice cream

Running a restaurant means going that extra mile—which sometimes includes helping staff in other departments. For example, at Farallon restaurant, Chris Durie, our general manager, is an honorary member of the pastry department. His love for sweets and exemplary palate have made him our prime recipe tester. Only when his eyes crinkle with pleasure do we know we have a dessert we can offer to our customers. I dedicate this dessert to Chris. Peppermint ice cream is a seasonal flavor for many ice cream companies. Now, you can make it at home all year-round. To crush peppermint candies, put them in a resealable plastic bag and crush with a rolling pin. If they are individually wrapped, crush first and then unwrap them.

SERVES
6

peppermint ice cream
¾ cup milk

2¼ cups heavy (whipping) cream

⅓ cup sugar

36 peppermint candies; 18 finely crushed, 18 coarsely crushed

Large pinch of kosher salt

chocolate crepes
1 cup milk

2 tablespoons unsweetened cocoa powder

2 large eggs

¼ cup sugar

½ cup all-purpose flour

⅛ teaspoon kosher salt

½ ounce (1 tablespoon) unsalted butter, melted, plus ¼ teaspoon for greasing pan

½ teaspoon vanilla extract

Cocoa Sauce, warmed (page 196)

TO MAKE THE ICE CREAM: Combine the milk, cream, sugar, finely crushed peppermint candies, and salt in a heavy saucepan. Cook over medium heat, stirring occasionally, until almost simmering. Pour the mixture into a bowl and cool over an ice bath until room temperature. Refrigerate the custard for at least 4 hours or up to overnight. Put the coarsely crushed peppermint pieces in a medium bowl and put it in the freezer.

Strain the custard, discarding the peppermint pieces. Churn in an ice cream machine according to the manufacturer's instructions. Fold the ice cream into the coarsely crushed peppermint pieces. Freeze the ice cream until scoopable, about 4 hours, depending on your freezer.

TO MAKE THE CREPES: In a food processor or blender, process the milk and the cocoa powder until smooth. Add the eggs and sugar and process until smooth. Add the flour and salt and process again until smooth. Mix in the 1 tablespoon melted butter and vanilla extract. Cover and refrigerate for 30 minutes.

Heat a 6-inch crepe or nonstick pan over medium heat. Lightly grease the bottom of the pan with the ¼ teaspoon butter. Pour about 2 tablespoons of the crepe batter into the pan, rotating the pan so that a thin layer covers the entire bottom. Cook for 1½ minutes. Using the tip of a knife, loosen an edge of the crepe from the pan. With your fingers, flip the crepe over and cook for another 15 seconds. Place the finished crepe on a large plate. Repeat, overlapping the crepes slightly to stack, to make at least 18 crepes. It is not necessary to grease the pan after making each crepe. Wrap the crepes in plastic wrap and store at room temperature until ready to use.

continued

flavor twist

mascarpone ice cream (PAGE 103)
OR
mexican chocolate
ice cream (PAGE 125)

TO SERVE: Fold the crepes into quarters. Place 3 crepes on each of 6 plates. Place a scoop of peppermint ice cream in the center. Pour some of the cocoa sauce over the ice cream. Serve extra sauce in a pitcher on the side.

IN ADVANCE: The crepes can be made 1 day ahead. Wrap in plastic wrap and refrigerate. They can also be frozen for up to 1 week. Wrap in plastic wrap.

gingerbread
with apple ice cream and calvados caramel sauce

Like other classic desserts such as angel food cake or vanilla ice cream, gingerbread is delicious eaten plain. But what makes a classic dessert so great is that you can dress it up for special occasions. Here, Calvados-flavored caramel and apple ice cream make this gingerbread a stellar dessert worthy of any white-tablecloth party.

SERVES
8

apple ice cream

4 (about 2 pounds) Golden Delicious apples

½ cup apple juice

¾ cup granulated sugar

1 tablespoon freshly squeezed lemon juice

⅛ teaspoon kosher salt

2 cups heavy (whipping) cream

1 cup milk

2-inch piece cinnamon stick

2 tablespoons Calvados or apple brandy

TO MAKE THE ICE CREAM: Peel, quarter, and core the apples. Slice them ⅛ inch thick and put them in a large sauté pan with the apple juice, sugar, lemon juice, and salt. Cook over medium-high heat, stirring occasionally, until the apples are very soft and all the liquid has evaporated, about 15 minutes. Purée the apples in a food processor and strain through a medium-mesh sieve. Let cool to room temperature.

Combine the cream, milk, and cinnamon stick in a saucepan. Cook over medium heat until almost simmering. Transfer to a bowl and cool over an ice bath until room temperature. Stir in the apple purée and Calvados or brandy. Refrigerate for at least 4 hours or up to overnight. Remove the cinnamon stick. Churn in an ice cream machine according to the manufacturer's instructions. Freeze until scoopable, about 4 hours, depending on your freezer.

continued

gingerbread

2½ cups all-purpose flour

¾ teaspoon baking soda

1 teaspoon ground ginger

¼ teaspoon kosher salt

6 ounces (12 tablespoons) unsalted
butter, softened

½ cup granulated sugar

⅓ cup firmly packed brown sugar

2 large eggs

½ cup unsulphured dark molasses

¾ cup sour cream

2 tablespoons grated fresh ginger

2 tablespoons finely chopped
candied ginger

Calvados Caramel Sauce, warmed
(page 201)

flavor twist

caramel ice cream (PAGE 90)
OR
pumpkin ice cream (PAGE 133)

TO MAKE THE GINGERBREAD: Preheat the oven to 350°F. Grease and flour a 9-by-13-inch baking pan. Sift together the flour, baking soda, and ground ginger. Add the salt. With an electric mixer, cream the butter and the granulated and brown sugars together until light and fluffy. Add the eggs one at a time, mixing well between each addition and scraping down the sides of the bowl. On low speed, add the molasses and then the sour cream. Stir in the grated ginger and then the dry ingredients. Spread the batter in the prepared pan. Sprinkle the candied ginger on top. Bake until a skewer inserted in the center comes out clean, about 30 minutes. Let cool to room temperature before cutting.

TO SERVE: Cut the gingerbread into 3-inch squares. (There will be extra gingerbread for breakfast the next day.) Place a piece of the gingerbread on each plate. Place a scoop of apple ice cream on top. Pour warm caramel sauce over the ice cream and cake. Serve immediately.

IN ADVANCE: The gingerbread is best baked and served the same day. Store at room temperature.

mango soup
with coconut sherbet and strawberry sorbet

Jen Creager and Terri Wu are the team that keeps the Farallon pastry department running like a well-buttered machine. No matter how much work there is to be done, baking with them is always lively and energizing. They orchestrate the production of all the cakes, glazes, doughs, cookies, chocolates, and sauces needed for the menu. They also create a daily *amuse-bouche* (French for "fun for the mouth") to offer to our customers as a preamble to dessert. It acts as a bridge for the taste buds between the main and dessert courses. When served in miniature portions, this recipe makes a great *amuse*. In bigger portions, it makes a light, refreshing dessert perfect after a heavier meal.

SERVES
6

coconut sherbet
1⅓ cups unsweetened coconut milk
1 cup coconut cream, such as Coco Lopez
1½ tablespoons granulated sugar

strawberry sorbet
1 pint fresh strawberries
½ cup sugar
¼ cup water
1 teaspoon freshly squeezed lemon juice
Large pinch of kosher salt

TO MAKE THE SHERBET: Whisk together the coconut milk, coconut cream, and sugar. Refrigerate for at least 1 hour. Churn in an ice cream machine according to the manufacturer's instructions. Freeze for several hours until scoopable, about 3 hours, depending on your freezer.

TO MAKE THE SORBET: Purée the strawberries in a food processor. Strain through a medium-mesh sieve, discarding the seeds. There should be about 1¼ cups purée. Stir together the strawberry purée, sugar, water, lemon juice, and salt. Refrigerate for at least 2 hours or up to overnight. Churn in an ice cream machine according to the manufacturer's instructions. Freeze until scoopable, about 4 hours, depending on your freezer.

continued

mango soup

4 ripe mangoes, peeled and pitted

1 cup freshly squeezed orange juice

⅓ cup water

⅔ cup sugar, plus more if needed

⅛ teaspoon kosher salt

2 teaspoons freshly squeezed lime juice

flavor twist

crème fraîche ice cream (PAGE 83)
AND
blackberry sorbet (PAGE 35),
OR
candied ginger ice cream (PAGE 64)
AND
cassis-berry sherbet (PAGE 109)

TO MAKE THE SOUP: Purée the mango flesh in a food processor. Strain through a medium-mesh sieve. In a bowl, whisk together the mango purée, orange juice, water, the ⅔ cup sugar, the salt, and lime juice. Taste for sweetness and add more sugar if necessary. Refrigerate until cold, about 1 hour.

TO SERVE: Pour some soup into each of 6 shallow bowls. Place a small scoop of coconut sherbet and strawberry sorbet in each bowl. Serve immediately.

IN ADVANCE: The sorbet and sherbet can be made 1 day in advance. For maximum flavor, the soup should be made the day you plan to serve the dessert. Keep refrigerated.

oat financiers
with peach ice cream

When I asked friends for their memories of homemade ice cream, the flavor that kept coming up was peach. Baby boomers like me fidgeted through the hand churning of the ice cream machine, but it was worth the wait. Often, the ice cream never made it to the freezer but disappeared behind stabbing spoons as it was devoured right from the canister. My family was generally orderly and gracious, but when it came to peach ice cream, it was survival of the fittest. Whoever got the dasher, usually the last person to crank, went quietly to a corner of the porch to savor it.

SERVES
8

peach ice cream

2 pounds ripe peaches

10 tablespoons sugar

Large pinch of kosher salt

½ teaspoon freshly squeezed lemon juice

1⅓ cups heavy (whipping) cream

½ cup milk

oat financiers

4 ounces (8 tablespoons) unsalted butter

⅔ cup (3 ounces) whole natural almonds, toasted (see page 17)

¾ cup confectioners' sugar

⅓ cup plus 2 tablespoons old-fashioned rolled oats

½ cup all-purpose flour

⅛ teaspoon kosher salt

4 large egg whites

½ cup granulated sugar

TO MAKE THE ICE CREAM: Peel, pit, and coarsely chop the peaches. Place them in a medium saucepan with 7 tablespoons of the sugar, the salt, and lemon juice. Cook over medium heat, stirring frequently, until jamlike in texture, about 20 minutes. Remove from the heat and let cool to room temperature.

Combine the cream, milk, and the remaining 3 tablespoons sugar in a medium saucepan. Cook over medium heat, stirring occasionally, until the liquid begins to bubble around the edges. Transfer to a bowl and cool over an ice bath until room temperature. Stir in the peaches and refrigerate for at least 4 hours or up to overnight. Churn in an ice cream machine according to the manufacturer's instructions. Freeze until scoopable, about 4 hours, depending on your freezer.

TO MAKE THE FINANCIERS: Preheat the oven to 350°F. Grease and flour a 9-by-13-inch baking pan. Tap out the excess flour. Melt the butter in a small saucepan. Cook over medium heat until it turns light brown in color. Strain through a fine-mesh sieve, discarding the solids, and let cool to room temperature. In a food processor, finely grind the almonds, confectioners' sugar, and the ⅓ cup oats. Transfer to a medium bowl. Stir in the flour and salt. In another bowl, whisk the egg whites lightly. Whisk in the granulated sugar until combined. Stir in the dry ingredients until blended. Whisk in the butter. Spread the batter in the pan. Sprinkle the remaining 2 tablespoons oats over the batter. Bake until a skewer inserted in the center comes out clean, about 20 minutes. Remove from the oven and let cool to room temperature.

4 fresh peaches

½ teaspoon freshly squeezed
lemon juice

About 2 tablespoons granulated
sugar, optional

flavor twist

vanilla malt ice cream (PAGE 119)
OR
blood orange sorbet (PAGE 165)

TO SERVE: Peel, pit, and cut the peaches into 1-inch pieces. Put the peaches in a bowl and taste for sweetness. Add the lemon juice and a little sugar if they are not sweet enough. Trim the edges of the financier cake. Cut the financier cake into 1¼-by-2¼-inch rectangles. Save scraps for nibbling. Place several pieces on a plate, slightly overlapping. Place some peaches next to the cake. Place a scoop of ice cream on top of the peaches. Serve immediately.

IN ADVANCE: The financiers can be made 1 day in advance. Cover with plastic wrap and store at room temperature.

pineapple upside-down cake
with passion fruit ice cream

Cake served with ice cream is a favorite in my house. Many people, my brother included, feel that cake is basically not worth its salt (or sugar) unless combined with a plump scoop of ice cream. Vanilla is the most popular flavor to pair with cakes, but other flavors can lend a dessert more dimension and kick. Here, passion fruit ice cream gives traditional pineapple upside-down cake a whole new life.

SERVES
8

passion fruit ice cream
6 large egg yolks

½ cup granulated sugar

⅛ teaspoon kosher salt

1¼ cups milk

1½ cups heavy (whipping) cream

5 tablespoons passion fruit purée (see page 18)

pineapple upside-down cake
1 small fresh pineapple

7 ounces (14 tablespoons) unsalted butter, softened

¾ cup firmly packed dark brown sugar

1 cup granulated sugar

2 large eggs

1⅔ cups all-purpose flour

2 teaspoons baking powder

½ teaspoon kosher salt

1 cup sour cream or crème fraîche

1 teaspoon vanilla extract

TO MAKE THE ICE CREAM: In a bowl, whisk together the egg yolks, ¼ cup of the sugar, and the salt. Combine the milk, cream, and remaining ¼ cup sugar in a heavy saucepan. Cook over medium heat, stirring occasionally, until almost simmering. Slowly pour the milk and cream into the eggs, whisking as you pour. Return the milk mixture to the saucepan. Cook over medium-low heat, stirring constantly with a heat-resistant plastic or wooden spatula, until the custard reaches 175°F and lightly coats the spatula.

Strain the custard into a clean bowl and cool over an ice bath until room temperature. Stir in the passion fruit purée. Refrigerate the custard for at least 4 hours or up to overnight. Churn in an ice cream machine according to the manufacturer's instructions. Freeze until scoopable, about 4 hours, depending on your freezer.

TO MAKE THE CAKE: Preheat the oven to 350°F. Peel, quarter, and core the pineapple. Cut the pineapple into 1-by-¾-inch pieces. You should have about 2¼ cups. Reserve any extra for another use. Melt 3 ounces (6 tablespoons) of the butter in a small saucepan. Whisk in the brown sugar and cook over medium-low heat until the sugar is mostly dissolved. Whisk until smooth. Pour the brown sugar mixture into the bottom of a 9-inch cake pan. Place the pineapple pieces in a single layer over the brown sugar mixture. In a large bowl, cream the remaining 4 ounces (8 tablespoons) butter and the granulated sugar together until smooth and fluffy. Stir in the eggs one at a time, beating well after each addition. Sift together the flour and baking powder and stir in the salt. In a small bowl, combine the sour cream or crème fraîche and vanilla extract. In 3 additions, alternately stir the wet and the dry ingredients into the butter mixture until well blended, scraping down the sides of the bowl periodically. Spread the batter over the pineapple. Bake until a skewer inserted in the center comes out clean, 50 to 55 minutes.

TO SERVE: Let the cake cool for 5 minutes. Run a small knife around the inside edge of the pan. Place a large plate on top of the cake. Invert the plate and cake pan together. Remove the cake pan. Scrape off any brown sugar topping that sticks to the pan and spread it over the pineapple. Serve the cake at room temperature, with the passion fruit ice cream.

IN ADVANCE: The cake is best eaten the day it is baked. Store at room temperature.

plum-cornmeal cake
with plum sorbet

For pastry chefs, ripe, juicy plums are the hidden jewels of summer fruits. Their color adds vibrancy to desserts. Adding sugar balances out their tartness and brings out their complex flavors. This cake is good enough to eat by itself (especially with coffee for breakfast!), but the plum sorbet gives it an added plum punch.

SERVES
8

plum sorbet

2 pounds (about 8) ripe red-fleshed plums, such as Santa Rosa

½ cup granulated sugar, plus more if needed

¼ cup water

Large pinch of kosher salt

1 teaspoon freshly squeezed lemon juice

plum-cornmeal cake

1½ cups all-purpose flour

1 teaspoon baking powder

⅛ teaspoon ground cinnamon

Large pinch of kosher salt

½ cup plus 1 tablespoon cornmeal

6 ounces (12 tablespoons) unsalted butter, softened

1 cup sugar

3 large eggs

⅓ cup milk

½ teaspoon freshly squeezed lemon juice

½ teaspoon vanilla extract

3 ripe red-fleshed plums, such as Santa Rosa

Chantilly Cream (page 205)

TO MAKE THE SORBET: Quarter the plums, discard the pits, and cut into ½-inch pieces. Purée the plums in a food processor until smooth. Strain the purée through a medium-mesh sieve into a medium bowl, discarding the skins. There should be about 2¾ cups purée. Stir in the ½ cup sugar, the water, salt, and lemon juice. Taste for sweetness and add a little more sugar if necessary. Refrigerate for at least 2 hours or up to overnight. Churn in an ice cream machine according to the manufacturer's instructions. Freeze until scoopable, about 4 hours, depending on your freezer.

TO MAKE THE CAKE: Preheat the oven to 350°F. Grease and flour a 9½-inch spring-form pan. Tap out the excess flour.

Sift the flour, baking powder, and cinnamon together in a bowl. Stir in the salt and the ½ cup cornmeal.

In a bowl, cream the butter and sugar until light and fluffy. Add the eggs one at a time, beating well after each addition. In a small bowl, stir together the milk, lemon juice, and vanilla extract. In 3 additions, alternately stir in the dry ingredients and the milk into the butter mixture just until combined. Spread half of the batter in the prepared pan. Place half of the plums over the cake batter. Repeat with the remaining cake batter and remaining plums. Sprinkle the 1 tablespoon corn-meal over the top of the cake. Bake until a skewer inserted in the center comes out clean, about 50 minutes. Cool to room temperature.

continued

flavor twist

· · · · · · · · · · ·

orange-cardamom
ice cream (PAGE 104)
OR
caramel ice cream (PAGE 90)

TO SERVE: Cut the cake into slices. Place a slice on each plate with some plum sorbet and Chantilly cream. Serve immediately.

IN ADVANCE: The cake tastes best prepared the day you plan to serve it, but it can be made a day ahead. Store at room temperature, well wrapped in plastic wrap.

ICE CREAM SHOP

profile

Sketch

1809 FOURTH STREET
BERKELEY, CALIFORNIA

MOTTO: "One of life's simpler pleasures."

YEAR OPENED: 2004.

OWNERS: Ruthie Planas and Eric Shelton.

HOW THE NAME WAS CHOSEN: A *sketch* is the beauty and purity of any idea.

NUMBER OF FLAVORS IN REPERTOIRE: Fifty-five to sixty.

MOST POPULAR FLAVORS: Sur del Lago chocolate, burnt caramel.

SIGNATURE FLAVORS: Straus Family Dairy yogurt, Yirgacheffe coffee, Earl Grey.

WHAT DO THEY DO WHEN IT GETS COLD OUT: Sell hot chocolate with ice cream in it.

AVAILABLE FOR SHIPPING: Sorry, you have to go there.

THE SCOOP: Ruthie and Eric are well-known pastry chefs in the San Francisco area. Tired of being cooped up in restaurant kitchens all day, they opened an ice cream shop on Berkeley's popular Fourth Street shopping promenade.

warm, gooey chocolate cakes
with chocolate–chocolate chunk ice cream

As a pastry chef, I see Americans' obsession with chocolate up close. As diners spot chocolate desserts on the menu, their eyes light up, they get a slight smile at the corners of their mouths, and they grip the menu a little tighter, as if afraid someone might try to take it away from them before they can order that dessert. Every dessert menu should include at least one chocolate dish. Some of the selections can have chocolate as only one of several elements, but at least one should be 100 percent chocolate, rich and intense. When I first put this offering on the menu I worried that it might be too chocolaty. I then remembered that for chocolate-lovers, there is no such state.

SERVES
6

chocolate–chocolate chunk ice cream
4 large egg yolks

½ cup sugar

⅛ teaspoon kosher salt

1⅔ cups whole milk

1⅔ cups heavy (whipping) cream

⅓ cup unsweetened cocoa powder

4 ounces bittersweet chocolate, coarsely chopped

chocolate cakes
6 ounces bittersweet chocolate, chopped

4 ounces (8 tablespoons) unsalted butter

2 tablespoons cake flour

⅓ cup unsweetened cocoa powder

¼ teaspoon kosher salt

3 large eggs

¾ cup granulated sugar

flavor twist

grand marnier ice cream (PAGE 185)
OR
multi-chocolate ice cream (PAGE 157)

TO MAKE THE ICE CREAM: In a bowl, whisk together the egg yolks, ¼ cup of the sugar, and the salt. Combine the milk, cream, and the remaining ¼ cup sugar in a heavy saucepan. Cook over medium heat, stirring occasionally, until almost simmering. Slowly whisk the milk and cream into the egg mixture. Whisk in the cocoa powder. Return the mixture to the saucepan. Cook over medium-low heat, stirring constantly, until the custard reaches 175°F and lightly coats the spatula.

Strain the custard into a clean bowl and cool over an ice bath until room temperature. Refrigerate the custard for at least 4 hours or up to overnight. Put the chocolate in a bowl and put the bowl in the freezer. Churn the ice cream in an ice cream machine according to the manufacturer's instructions. Fold the ice cream into the chocolate. Freeze until scoopable, about 4 hours, depending on your freezer.

TO MAKE THE CAKES: Preheat the oven to 325°F. Butter and sugar the insides of six 4-ounce ramekins. Tap out the excess sugar.

Melt the chocolate and the butter together in a double boiler over hot water. Stir until combined. Sift the cake flour and cocoa powder together in a bowl. Stir in the salt. In a large bowl, whisk together the eggs and sugar until combined. Whisk in the chocolate mixture. Fold in the dry ingredients.

Divide the batter among the prepared ramekins. Place the ramekins in a 9-by-13-inch baking pan. Fill the pan with hot water to halfway up the sides of the ramekins. Carefully put the pan in the oven and bake until the cakes are no longer wet looking, are slightly firm when pressed on top, and just beginning to crack, about 35 minutes. Let the cakes cool slightly.

TO SERVE: Serve the cakes warm, in the ramekins. If necessary, reheat in a preheated 350°F oven for 5 minutes. Top with a scoop of ice cream.

IN ADVANCE: The cakes can be made 1 day in advance. Store at room temperature, wrapped in plastic wrap.

warm blueberry filo stacks
with grand marnier ice cream

Desserts need a contrast of textures. Because flavor takes longer to register to your brain, texture is the first thing you notice when you take a bite of a dessert, making that all-important first impression. Here, the crispness of filo balances the cool richness of ice cream. Like the yin and yang of Chinese philosophy, they are opposites that work together to create a balanced and tasty dessert.

grand marnier ice cream
6 large egg yolks

¾ cup sugar

¼ teaspoon kosher salt

2 cups milk

2½ cups heavy (whipping) cream

Zest stripped from 2 oranges

3 tablespoons Grand Marnier

pecan filo squares
⅓ cup (1½ ounces) pecans, toasted (see page 17)

3 tablespoons sugar

Four 11-by-17-inch sheets thawed frozen filo (see page 17)

1½ ounces (3 tablespoons) unsalted butter, melted

Blueberry Sauce, warmed (page 193)

TO MAKE THE ICE CREAM: In a bowl, whisk together the egg yolks, ¼ cup of the sugar, and the salt. Combine the milk, cream, the remaining ½ cup sugar, and the orange zest in a heavy saucepan. Cook over medium heat, stirring occasionally, until almost simmering. Turn off the heat and cover the pan. Let the orange zest infuse for 10 minutes. Slowly whisk the orange cream into the egg mixture. Return the orange cream mixture to the saucepan. Cook over medium-low heat, stirring constantly with a heat-resistant plastic or wooden spatula, until the custard reaches 175°F and lightly coats the spatula.

Transfer to a clean bowl. Cool over an ice bath until room temperature. Strain the custard into a clean bowl, discarding the orange zest, and stir in the Grand Marnier. Refrigerate the custard for at least 4 hours or up to overnight. Churn in an ice cream machine according to the manufacturer's instructions. Freeze until scoopable, about 4 hours, depending on your freezer.

TO MAKE THE FILO SQUARES: Preheat the oven to 375°F. Line 2 baking sheets with parchment paper.

Finely grind the pecans and the sugar in a food processor and put in a small bowl. Lay the filo sheets on a work surface. Remove one sheet of filo and place it on the work surface. Cover the stack of filo with a kitchen towel. Brush the single sheet with one fourth of the melted butter and sprinkle with a quarter of the pecan mixture.

Place a second sheet of filo on top and butter and sugar it in the same way. Repeat with 2 more layers of filo, buttering and sugaring each one. Cut the filo into 3-inch squares. There should be 16 squares. Place the squares on the prepared pans. Bake until golden brown, about 15 minutes. Cool to room temperature.

continued

flavor twist

brown sugar ice cream (PAGE 127)
OR
butter pecan ice cream (PAGE 40)

TO SERVE: Place a filo square on each of 8 plates. Place a scoop of ice cream on top of the filo. Spoon some warm blueberry sauce over the ice cream. Place a second piece of filo on top. Serve immediately.

IN ADVANCE: Prepare the filo squares the day you plan to serve the dessert. Leave them on the baking sheets and wrap in plastic wrap. Store at room temperature.

frozen hazelnut parfaits
filled with hot fudge sauce

India has the delightful custom of serving a bite or two of dessert when the savory meal is presented, teasing your taste buds with a preview of coming attractions. You can do the same. When you hollow out the center of the parfaits to make room for the hot chocolate sauce, place the scraps in small cups or bowls to serve with your main course.

SERVES
8

¾ cup (3½ ounces) hazelnuts, toasted and skinned (see pages 17–18)

6 large egg yolks

⅔ cup sugar

Large pinch of kosher salt

2 tablespoons freshly squeezed orange juice

2 tablespoons hazelnut liqueur (Frangelico) or rum

2 cups heavy (whipping) cream

½ teaspoon vanilla extract

Hot Fudge Sauce, warmed (page 198)

TO MAKE THE PARFAITS: Place 8 ring molds (3 inches high and 2 inches in diameter) or similar-sized paper or plastic cups onto a parchment-paper-lined baking sheet. Grind the hazelnuts medium fine in a food processor.

In a stainless-steel bowl, whisk together the egg yolks, sugar, salt, orange juice, and hazelnut liqueur or rum until smooth. Place the bowl over a saucepan of rapidly simmering water, making sure the water is not touching the bottom of the bowl. Whisk until slightly thickened, about 3 minutes. Put the mixture in the bowl of an electric mixer and whip on medium-high speed until room temperature. In a bowl, whip the cream and the vanilla until soft peaks form. Fold the cream and the ground hazelnuts into the cooled egg mixture.

Using an ice cream scoop, fill the ring molds with the mousse. Freeze until half-frozen, about 1 hour. Using a small ice cream scoop or melon baller, scoop out about 2 tablespoons of parfait from each mold. Save the scraps for nibbling. Continue to freeze until hard, another 2 to 3 hours, depending on your freezer.

TO SERVE: Carefully run a knife around the inside edge of each frozen parfait. Unmold and place on individual plates. Fill each of the holes with hot fudge sauce. Serve immediately, with extra sauce on the side.

IN ADVANCE: The parfaits can be made, unmolded, and returned to the freezer, for up to 3 days. Place on a baking pan and wrap well in plastic wrap. Fill with hot fudge sauce just before serving.

profiteroles
with orange custard–
chocolate chip ice
cream and bittersweet
chocolate sauce

Friends and customers often scribble down the names of their
favorite ice cream spots around the country on business cards and cocktail
napkins and send them to me. While I *did* make it to Des Moines to try the peppermint at Bauder's Pharmacy (it was fabulous), there is no way I can visit them all. I
was able to try quite a few once I discovered you can place orders online at many places
and have the ice cream shipped overnight on dry ice. This is not the cheapest way to
buy ice cream, but it comes well packed and frozen. One of my favorites was the
orange custard–chocolate chip ice cream from the University Creamery at Penn
State; it was the inspiration for this dessert.

SERVES
8

orange custard–chocolate
chip ice cream

5 large egg yolks

¾ cup sugar

¼ teaspoon kosher salt

2¼ cups milk

2¼ cups heavy (whipping) cream

Zest stripped from 2 oranges

**5 ounces bittersweet chocolate,
chopped to chip size**

TO MAKE THE ICE CREAM: In a bowl, whisk together the egg yolks, ¼ cup of the
sugar, and the salt. Combine the milk, cream, orange zest, and remaining ½ cup
sugar in a heavy saucepan. Cook over medium heat, stirring occasionally, until
almost simmering. Slowly pour the milk and cream into the egg mixture, whisking
together as you pour. Return the mixture to the saucepan. Cook over medium-low
heat, stirring constantly with a heat-resistant plastic or wooden spatula, until the
custard reaches 175°F and lightly coats the spatula.

Transfer to a clean bowl. Cool over an ice bath until room temperature. Strain and
refrigerate the custard for at least 4 hours or up to overnight. Put the chocolate in a
bowl and put the bowl in the freezer. Churn in an ice cream machine according to
the manufacturer's instructions. Put the ice cream in the bowl with the chocolate
chips and fold together until the chips are evenly distributed. Freeze until scoopable, about 4 hours, depending on your freezer.

profiteroles

¾ cup water

⅛ teaspoon kosher salt

3 ounces (6 tablespoons) unsalted butter

1 tablespoon granulated sugar

¾ cup all-purpose flour

3 large eggs

Bittersweet Chocolate Sauce, warmed (page 200)

flavor twist

banana ice cream (PAGE 155)
OR
peppermint ice cream (PAGE 169)

TO MAKE THE PROFITEROLES: Preheat the oven to 400°F. Line 2 baking sheets with parchment paper.

Combine the water, salt, butter, and sugar in a saucepan. Bring the mixture to a full boil over medium heat. Remove the pan from the heat and stir in the flour. Return the pan to the heat and cook, stirring constantly, for 2 minutes. Put the dough in the bowl of an electric mixer and let cool for a few minutes until steam no longer rises from it. Beating on medium-low speed, add the eggs one at a time, beating well after each addition. Place spoonfuls of the dough, each about the size of a half dollar, 2 inches apart on the prepared pans. There should be at least 24 profiteroles.

Bake for 10 minutes, then reduce the heat to 350°F. Continue to bake until a deep golden brown, about 25 minutes. Remove from the oven and cut a slit in the side of each profiterole. Turn off the oven and return them to the oven for 5 minutes to dry out. Let cool to room temperature.

TO SERVE: Cut each profiterole in half horizontally and place 3 bottoms on each of 8 plates. Place a scoop of ice cream in each bottom piece. Place the tops of the profiteroles on the ice cream. Pour some chocolate sauce over and around the profiteroles. Serve immediately. Serve extra chocolate sauce in a pitcher.

IN ADVANCE: The profiteroles should be baked the same day they are eaten. Unbaked but formed profiteroles can be frozen for up to 1 week. Wrap the baking sheets in plastic wrap. Let sit at room temperature for 20 minutes and then bake. Allow an extra 5 minutes for baking.

An adornment adds beauty and decorates an object. What better description for the multitude of wonderful goodies we can load onto our ice cream? Ice cream is gratifying by itself, but drizzle Coffee Caramel Sauce or Hot Fudge Sauce on it, or sprinkle it with Nutty Nuts or Candied Coconut, and you turn enjoyment into pleasure, pleasure into ecstasy. Canned, bottled, and processed garnishes will disappear from your pantry as these recipes become part of your recipe collection.

Are you entertaining last-minute guests or running short on time? Pick up some good ice cream at a local ice cream shop, add a homemade touch like Very Cherry Cherries or Roasted Pineapple, and everyone will happily indulge and beg for seconds.

I have made suggestions here for using these recipes with specific desserts in this book, but feel free to let your imagination and taste buds run wild as you concoct your own combinations. The possibilities are endless. Whoever said it was possible to have too much of a good thing wasn't talking about adorning ice cream.

ADORNMENTS

berry sauce

Raspberries and blackberries make delicious and versatile sauces. But their flavor is quite pronounced, so you must be careful the sauce does not overpower the dessert. Generally, the lighter the dessert, the more sparing you should be with the sauce. I usually use frozen berries for sauce, even in summer. They are a lot less expensive. If you have crushed or less-than-perfect fresh berries, by all means use them.

MAKES ABOUT
3
CUPS

4 pints fresh or 48 ounces thawed no-sugar-added frozen raspberries, blackberries, or a mixture

½ teaspoon freshly squeezed lemon juice

Large pinch of kosher salt

6 tablespoons sugar, plus more as needed

Purée the berries in a food processor until smooth. Strain through a medium-mesh sieve, discarding the seeds. There should be about 2 cups purée. Stir in the lemon juice, salt, and the 6 tablespoons sugar. Taste for sweetness and add more sugar if necessary. Cover and refrigerate until ready to serve.

IN ADVANCE: The sauce can be made 2 days in advance.

blueberry
sauce

$1\frac{1}{2}$

CUPS

Fresh blueberries are crucial in this sauce. Frozen blueberries are too runny and watery. A little trick to give this sauce texture is to add half of the blueberries later in the cooking process.

3 pints fresh blueberries

½ cup sugar

1 teaspoon freshly squeezed lemon juice

Large pinch of kosher salt

Put half of the blueberries and all of the remaining ingredients in a medium saucepan. Cook over medium heat, stirring frequently, until the blueberries become mostly liquid and the sugar dissolves, about 5 minutes. Add the remaining blueberries and continue to cook just until they break open and are warmed through, about 2 minutes. Serve warm or cold.

IN ADVANCE: The sauce can be made up to 3 days in advance. Cover and refrigerate. If serving warm, reheat in a double boiler or microwave.

butterscotch **sauce**

When Heather Ames, Farallon's lunch chef, got married, we had a party at the restaurant. I offered to make a cake, but she preferred something simpler. With that in mind, Jen Creager, Terri Wu, and I created an extensive sundae bar in a serve-yourself buffet. Containers of chocolate, coffee, vanilla, and butter crunch ice cream were surrounded by bowls of Red Wine–Roasted Strawberries (page 152), Roasted Pineapple (page 210), and Nutty Nuts (page 212), along with this sauce. Cake is a great way to commemorate an occasion, but this simple alternative was just as delicious and made the event more lively and memorable.

MAKES
1½
CUPS

3 ounces (6 tablespoons) unsalted butter
1⅓ cups firmly packed brown sugar
¾ cup corn syrup
5 tablespoons heavy (whipping) cream

Combine all the ingredients in a medium, heavy saucepan. Bring to a boil over medium-high heat and cook, stirring occasionally, until it thickens slightly, about 3 minutes. Remove from the heat and cool slightly before serving.

IN ADVANCE: The sauce can be made 1 week in advance. Cover and refrigerate.

ICE CREAM SHOP
profile

Babcock's Ice Cream

BABCOCK HALL
1605 LINDEN DRIVE
MADISON, WISCONSIN

MOTTO: None. In their area, everyone knows the reputation of their ice cream. It speaks for itself.
YEAR OPENED: 1951.
OWNER: University of Wisconsin.
HOW THE NAME WAS CHOSEN: Professor Babcock developed the industry standard for testing the butterfat level in ice cream.
NUMBER OF FLAVORS IN REPERTOIRE: Two hundred; twenty-five on hand monthly.
MOST POPULAR FLAVORS: Vanilla, chocolate truffle, cookie dough.
SIGNATURE FLAVORS: Orange custard–chocolate chip and Crazy Legs (named for local football legend El Roy Hirsh: red-colored vanilla ice cream with chocolate-coated football-shaped caramels); peppermint during the winter.
AVAILABLE FOR SHIPPING: www.wisconsinmade.com.
THE SCOOP: The ice cream shop provides a learning laboratory for research and instruction. September is the busiest month, as students and parents line up after being gone all summer.

chunky strawberry
sauce

Sometimes, you don't want a smooth sauce; you want little chunks to give it more personality. As always, taste the sauce for sweetness before adding all the sugar, as the sweetness of strawberries can vary.

2 pints fresh strawberries, hulled

¼ cup sugar, plus more if needed

2 teaspoons freshly squeezed lemon juice

Large pinch of kosher salt

Cut two thirds of the berries into quarters and purée them in a food processor until smooth. Strain through a medium-mesh sieve, discarding the seeds. Cut the remaining berries into ½-inch pieces. Stir them into the purée along with the ¼ cup sugar, lemon juice, and salt. Taste for sweetness. Add more sugar if necessary. Cover and refrigerate until ready to serve.

IN ADVANCE: The sauce can be made 2 days in advance.

cocoa
sauce

This sauce is low in fat, since there isn't any cream or chocolate. But be aware that if you use Vahlrona cocoa powder, which is the favorite of most pastry chefs, the fat content will be higher than with other varieties. Most chocolate sauces should be served warm, but this one is also terrific served cold.

MAKES ABOUT
2½
CUPS

1½ cups sugar

2 cups water

1 cup unsweetened cocoa powder

Stir the sugar and 1 cup of the water together in a medium saucepan. Bring to a boil over medium heat and cook for about 15 seconds until the sugar is dissolved.

In a small bowl, whisk together the cocoa powder and remaining 1 cup water. Whisk the cocoa mixture into the sugar mixture. Return to a boil and reduce the heat to a simmer. Cook, stirring occasionally, until the sauce thickens slightly, about 10 minutes. Remove from the heat and let cool to room temperature. Cover and refrigerate until ready to use.

IN ADVANCE: The sauce can be made 1 week in advance. Rewarm gently over low heat to serve warm.

Clockwise from top left: Bittersweet Chocolate Sauce (page 200), Blueberry Sauce (page 193), Berry Sauce (page 192), Classic Caramel Sauce (page 203), and Chunky Strawberry Sauce (page 195).

hot fudge
sauce

My grandmother (and namesake) used to make this sauce for my cousins and me when we were kids. Served hot, it gets chewy and fudgy when it hits the ice cream, but it doesn't stick to your teeth. Some of my relatives have different renditions, but my Aunt Joan remembered the original, and together we were able to record it for future generations. My entire extended family has tried this recipe for historical accuracy.

MAKES

2

CUPS

4 ounces unsweetened chocolate, coarsely chopped

4 ounces (8 tablespoons) unsalted butter, cut into 1-inch pieces

½ cup half-and-half

1½ cups sugar

Melt the chocolate and the butter together in a double boiler over simmering water. Whisk until smooth. Pour in the half-and-half in a steady stream, whisking as you pour. It's okay if it looks curdled. Slowly add ½ cup of the sugar in a steady stream, whisking as you pour. Continue stirring until the sugar has dissolved and isn't grainy, about 30 seconds. Add another ½ cup of sugar and again stir until it is dissolved and no longer grainy. Add the remaining ½ cup sugar in the same manner.

Cover the pan and cook, stirring occasionally, until the sauce becomes glossy and thickens slightly, about 25 minutes.

Serve warm. If not serving right away, put the sauce in a bowl and press plastic wrap directly onto the surface. This will prevent a skin from forming. The sauce will get grainy when cold but will become smooth when reheated. It can be reheated slowly in a double boiler or microwave.

IN ADVANCE: The sauce can be made up to 1 week in advance. Cover and refrigerate.

white chocolate
sauce

This sauce is a beautiful contrast served over dark or colorful ice creams or sorbets like raspberry, coffee, or chocolate. When made from some varieties of white chocolate, the sauce may come out a little thin. If that's the case, serve it straight from the refrigerator.

MAKES ABOUT
2
CUPS

1 cup heavy (whipping) cream

10 ounces white chocolate, finely chopped

Heat the cream in a saucepan over medium heat until it begins to bubble around the edges. Turn off the heat and add the chocolate. Cover the pot and let sit for 5 minutes. Whisk until smooth. Let cool to room temperature and then cover and refrigerate. Serve at room temperature or cold.

IN ADVANCE: The chocolate sauce can be made up to 2 weeks in advance. Cover and refrigerate.

bittersweet chocolate **sauce**

This sauce should always be in your refrigerator. It can be used over ice cream and also as a side sauce for cakes or mixed with milk to make hot chocolate. (I have even been known to sneak a spoonful right out of the container as an afternoon sweet snack.) Experiment with several brands of chocolate for the sauce, because this affects the final taste.

MAKES ABOUT
2
CUPS

1½ cups heavy (whipping) cream

10 ounces bittersweet chocolate, finely chopped

Heat the cream in a saucepan over medium heat until it begins to bubble around the edges. Turn off the heat and add the chocolate. Cover the pan and let sit for 5 minutes. Whisk until smooth. Let cool slightly and use now, or let cool to room temperature and refrigerate. The sauce is best served warm. It can be reheated in a double boiler or microwave.

IN ADVANCE: The chocolate sauce can be made up to 2 weeks in advance. Cover and refrigerate.

calvados caramel **sauce**

Adding Calvados to caramel sauce gives it a little kick. This sauce doesn't have a strong alcohol taste; it's more of a finesse flavor. Since long-aged Calvados can be expensive, if you aren't a Calvados sipper, use less-expensive apple brandy.

MAKES ABOUT
3
CUPS

2 cups sugar

½ cup water

1½ cups heavy (whipping) cream

3 tablespoons Calvados or apple brandy

⅛ teaspoon kosher salt

2 ounces (4 tablespoons) unsalted butter, softened

Stir the sugar and water together in a heavy saucepan. Cook over medium-high heat until the sugar dissolves, about 2 minutes. Increase the heat to high and continue to cook, without stirring, until the sugar is medium amber in color. Remove the pot from the heat and slowly stir in about ¼ cup of the cream. (Stir carefully, as the caramel will sputter as the cream is added.) Continue gradually stirring in the cream until it has all been added.

Let the caramel cool to room temperature, stirring occasionally, until warm. Stir in the Calvados or brandy and salt. Add the butter into the caramel in 4 additions, whisking each in completely before adding another piece.

Let cool, cover and refrigerate until ready to serve. If serving warm, reheat in a double boiler or microwave.

IN ADVANCE: The caramel sauce can be made up to 2 weeks ahead. Refrigerate until ready to reheat.

chocolate–peanut butter sauce

MAKES ABOUT
2
CUPS

This sauce could actually be a dessert on its own. When I first made it, I was barely able to ladle it over the ice cream because we kept digging our spoons directly into the saucepan. After I had rapped everyone's knuckles to get them away from the stove, we were able to sit down at the table like civilized people and pass the ice cream and sauce around. When we had all served ourselves, I noticed we had each taken, myself included, little scoops of ice cream and big ladles full of sauce. It turns out ice cream is just an excuse for the sauce. Natural peanut butter works best, as it is less sweet than commercial brands.

1¼ cups heavy (whipping) cream

8 ounces bittersweet chocolate, finely chopped

¼ cup creamy natural peanut butter

Heat the cream in a saucepan over medium heat until it begins to bubble around the edges. Turn off the heat and add the chocolate. Cover the pan and let sit for 5 minutes. Add the peanut butter and whisk until smooth.

Let cool slightly and serve. It can be reheated in a double boiler or microwave. Note: To serve the sauce cold, add another ½ cup cream.

IN ADVANCE: The sauce can be made up to 2 weeks in advance. Cover and refrigerate.

classic caramel **sauce**

Adding butter gives this old favorite a velvety texture. It should be added once the sauce has cooled a bit so that it emulsifies rather than melting into the sauce.

MAKES ABOUT
4
CUPS

3 cups sugar

1 cup water

2 cups heavy (whipping) cream

2 ounces (4 tablespoons) unsalted butter, softened

Large pinch of kosher salt

Stir the sugar and water together in a heavy saucepan. Cook over medium heat until the sugar dissolves, about 2 minutes. Increase to high heat and continue to cook, without stirring, until the sugar has caramelized and is medium amber in color. Remove the pan from the heat and slowly stir in about ¼ cup of the cream. (The caramel will sputter as the water is added, so stir carefully.) Continue gradually stirring in the remaining cream.

Let the caramel cool, stirring occasionally, until warm. Whisk in the butter and salt. Cover and refrigerate until ready to serve. If serving warm, reheat in a double boiler or microwave.

IN ADVANCE: The caramel sauce can be made up to 2 weeks ahead.

coffee caramel **sauce**

This sauce is one of my favorites. Ever since I first made it, it has been a pastry staple both at the restaurant and at home. It has the traditional caramel taste we all love, with rich coffee undertones. It adds another dimension to many desserts without making them too sweet. It's especially good with Brown Sugar Ice Cream Chocolate Roulade (page 127) or Brown Sugar Oat Wafers with Candied Ginger Ice Cream (page 64).

MAKES
2
CUPS

1 cup sugar

3 tablespoons water

⅓ cup brewed decaffeinated coffee

⅓ cup heavy (whipping) cream

2 ounces (4 tablespoons) unsalted butter, cut into 1-inch pieces and softened

⅛ teaspoon kosher salt

Stir the sugar and water together in a heavy saucepan. Cook over medium heat until the sugar dissolves, about 2 minutes. Increase to high heat and continue to cook, without stirring, until the sugar has caramelized and is medium amber in color. While the sugar is cooking, mix together the coffee and cream in a bowl. Remove the pan from the heat and slowly stir in about ¼ cup of the coffee-and-cream mixture. (The caramel will sputter as it is added, so stir carefully.) Continue gradually stirring in the mixture until all has been added. Let the caramel cool, stirring occasionally, until warm. Whisk in the butter and salt.

Cover and refrigerate until ready to serve. If serving warm, reheat in a double boiler or microwave.

IN ADVANCE: The coffee caramel sauce can be made up to 2 weeks ahead.

chantilly cream

I would be lost without Chantilly cream. Generous dollops of it on a dessert that didn't come out quite right can turn the dessert into a triumph. Served on the side, it can lighten an overly rich dessert. Use organic cream if you can find it, and stay away from ultrapasteurized cream, which is harder to whip to the perfect consistency. Always store Chantilly cream in the refrigerator, tightly covered. It picks up unpleasant odors easily.

MAKES ABOUT
3
CUPS

1½ cups heavy (whipping) cream

3 tablespoons sugar

½ teaspoon vanilla extract, seeds from ½ vanilla bean, or ½ teaspoon vanilla powder

Whisk the cream, sugar, and whichever vanilla you are using in a large bowl until soft peaks form. The cream should be thick but still satiny in appearance and never grainy.

IN ADVANCE: Chantilly cream can be whipped a couple of hours in advance, covered, and refrigerated. It may become a little loose as it sits. Just before serving, whip briefly with a whisk.

brown butter
tuile cups

Pastry chefs use tuile cookies primarily as a garnish, sculpting them into spirals, palm trees, sailboats, or even 3-D mobiles, and putting them on cakes, trifles, and even pieces of pie. I have seen enough of these silly decorations to last a lifetime. One of the ways tuiles do make a tasty contribution to dessert, however, is formed into cups to hold scoops of your favorite ice creams and sorbets. The light, crisp cookie complements the smooth, creamy consistency of the frozen sweet. Browning the butter gives it an added nutty flavor.

MAKES
12
TUILE CUPS

4 ounces (8 tablespoons) unsalted butter

3 large egg whites

¾ cup sugar

½ teaspoon vanilla extract

¾ cup all-purpose flour

¼ teaspoon salt

Preheat the oven to 350°F. Line 2 baking sheets with parchment paper.

Melt the butter in a small saucepan over medium heat and cook until light brown in color. Strain through a fine-mesh sieve, discarding the solids, and let cool to room temperature.

Whisk the egg whites in a medium bowl until frothy. Whisk in the sugar. Stir in the melted butter and vanilla. Stir in the flour and salt to make a smooth batter.

For each cookie, place 1 heaping tablespoon of batter on one of the prepared pans and spread the batter with the back of a spoon into a 6-inch round. Repeat making the other tuiles in the same manner, spacing them 1 inch apart. Bake, one tray at a time, until golden brown, about 7 minutes. Invert a small bowl (about 3¾ inches in diameter across the top and about 1¾ inches across the bottom, such as a custard cup) on the countertop. Using a metal spatula, remove a cookie from the baking sheet and place it upside down over the bottom of the bowl. With a towel or oven mitt to protect your hands, gently press the cookie so that it molds over the bowl. Hold for a couple of seconds. Carefully remove the cookie and place it right side up. Repeat with the other cookies. (If the cookies crack as you try to form them over the bowl, they have gotten too cool. Place in the oven for a minute to rewarm them.)

IN ADVANCE: The tuile cups can be made a day or two in advance. Store in an airtight container at room temperature.

candied
coconut

This coconut garnish goes with just about any ice cream or sorbet flavor. Use it along with some chocolate sauce to dress up Coffee Meringues with Coconut Ice Cream (page 68) into a plated dessert.

MAKES
2
CUPS

1 large egg white

¼ cup sugar

Large pinch of kosher salt

½ teaspoon vanilla extract

2 cups unsweetened flake coconut
(see page 16)

Preheat the oven to 350°F. In a medium bowl, whisk together the egg white, sugar, salt, and vanilla extract until blended. Gently stir in the coconut. Spread the coconut in a single layer on a baking sheet. Bake for 8 minutes, then stir the coconut with a metal spatula. Continue to bake until golden brown, about 5 minutes.

IN ADVANCE: The coconut can be prepared up to 1 week in advance. Store in an airtight container at room temperature.

praline

MAKES

3

CUPS

When making praline for ice cream, keep in mind a couple of tricks. If you want large pieces, make sure to use plenty of nuts, as in this recipe, so it will be easy to eat—you don't want the caramel pieces sticking to your teeth. If you prefer fewer nuts, chop the praline more finely, or better yet use a food processor.

1⅓ cups (6 ounces) nuts, such as almonds, hazelnuts, walnuts, macadamia, pecans, pistachios, or any combination

1½ cups sugar

¼ cup water

Preheat the oven to 350°F. Spread the nuts on a baking sheet and toast for 10 minutes. If you are using hazelnuts, remove the skins (see page 18).

Stir the sugar and water together in a heavy saucepan. Cook over medium-high heat until the sugar dissolves, about 2 minutes. Increase to high heat and continue to cook, not stirring, until the sugar has caramelized and is medium amber in color. Remove the pan from the heat and carefully stir in the nuts.

Spread the praline on a buttered baking sheet, separating the nuts into a single layer. Let cool until hard, about 1 hour. Break into coarse pieces or coarsely grind in a food processor using on-off pulses.

IN ADVANCE: Praline can be made at least 1 week in advance in nonhumid areas. Store in an airtight container. If the weather is humid, the praline will not last as long and will get sticky.

roasted pineapple

Don't limit serving pineapple with ice cream solely to banana splits. Pineapple is a great topping for a bowl of ginger, coconut, or crème fraîche ice cream. It also makes a nice garnish for Pineapple–Dark Rum Granita with Ginger Beer Sabayon (page 56), and it can be substituted for plums in Plum-Cornmeal Cake (page 181) for a wintertime version of that dessert.

MAKES ABOUT

2½

CUPS

One 3-pound fresh pineapple, peeled

¾ cup sugar

1 teaspoon corn syrup

¼ cup water

½ vanilla bean, halved lengthwise and seeds scraped out

Preheat the oven to 350°F. Lay the pineapple on its side and cut it into ¾-inch-thick rounds. Cut out the core in the center of each. Cut each ring into 8 pieces.

In a small saucepan, stir the sugar, corn syrup, water, and vanilla bean and seeds together. Cook over medium-high heat for 1 minute and brush down the sides with a pastry brush dipped in water. Continue to cook until light golden in color, 3 to 5 minutes. Pour into a 9-by-13-inch pan. Place the pineapple pieces in the pan in a single layer.

Bake for 20 minutes. Turn the pineapple over and continue to bake until golden brown, 45 minutes more.

IN ADVANCE: The pineapple can be roasted 1 day in advance. Cover and refrigerate, but bring to room temperature or warm before serving.

preserved
cherries

These cherries can pack a wallop, depending on which alcohol you use. Red wine or a fruity port produces mellower cherries, while vodka or a tannic port gives them a powerful flavor. Both are good; it just depends what your taste buds prefer. These are delicious served with a little bit of the liquid over practically any flavor of ice cream, or in Summertime Spumoni (page 119).

MAKES

4

CUPS

1 pound fresh Bing cherries, stemmed

2 cups port, red wine, or vodka

⅔ cup sugar

1 cinnamon stick

1 heaping tablespoon chopped candied ginger

Zest stripped from 1 lemon

Leave the pits in the cherries. In a bowl, stir together the port, red wine, or vodka and the sugar until the sugar is dissolved. Put the cherries in a bowl and pour the red wine over them. Add the cinnamon stick, ginger, and lemon zest. Cover and refrigerate for 2 weeks to 1 month. Remove the pits before eating.

IN ADVANCE: These cherries will last for up to 1 month in the refrigerator.

nutty
nuts

Nuts offer texture to an ice cream dessert. The contrast between the cool, smooth, creamy ice cream and the crunchy nuts wakes up all your taste buds. Nuts also cut the richness of ice cream. Nut-flavored ice creams, like butter pecan or maple walnut, don't offer the same contrast—the nuts need to be sprinkled on top of and around the dessert. Coating them with sugar and corn syrup and baking them makes them extra crunchy and a little bit sweet so they blend well with the dessert.

MAKES ABOUT
1½
CUPS

¼ cup sugar

2 tablespoons water

1 tablespoon corn syrup

Large pinch of kosher salt

1½ cups (7 ounces) almonds, skinned hazelnuts, macadamias, walnuts, pecans, pistachios, or any combination

Preheat the oven to 350°F. Stir together the sugar, water, corn syrup, and salt in a small saucepan. Bring to a boil over medium-high heat. Turn off the heat. Stir in the nuts until completely coated. Spread in a single layer in a baking pan. Bake for 5 minutes and gently stir the nuts. Continue to bake until golden brown, about 8 minutes more. Let cool and then store in an airtight container.

IN ADVANCE: Nutty Nuts can be made up to 1 week in advance.

very cherry
cherries

This sauce is an excellent way to extend the cherry season, because it lasts for weeks in your refrigerator. You can also preserve the sauce to make it last all year long. Make this when there is a plethora of cherries in the market and the price is low. Be sure to use a large pan so the sauce doesn't boil over. Pitting the cherries later in the recipe helps to preserve their shape; cooking with the pits also increases their flavor.

MAKES ABOUT

3

CUPS

2½ cups sugar

¾ cup water

1½ pounds fresh Bing cherries, stemmed

1½ teaspoons freshly squeezed lemon juice

⅛ teaspoon kosher salt

In a medium pan, stir together the sugar and water. Bring to a boil over medium heat and cook until the sugar is dissolved and the liquid is clear, about 1 minute. Stir in the cherries and bring back to a low boil. Simmer until the cherries are slightly shriveled and the liquid is red, about 5 minutes. Drain the cherries, reserving the liquid, and place them in a baking pan in a single layer. Let the cherries cool to room temperature. While they are cooling, return the reserved liquid to the pan and cook over medium heat to reduce until slightly syrupy, about 2 cups. Stir in the lemon juice and salt. Remove from the heat and let cool to room temperature.

Remove the pits from the cherries by gently squeezing each one. The pit will pop out. Gently stir the cherries into the sauce. Cover and refrigerate.

IN ADVANCE: The cherry sauce can be made up to 2 weeks in advance. Bring to room temperature or warm in a microwave before serving.

flavor reference chart

sources

Knowing where to find something takes much of the hassle out of shopping. Listed below are ice cream and general pastry equipment and ingredient sources with addresses, phone numbers, and web sites whenever appropriate. The Internet is extremely convenient, but brick-and-mortar stores are fun and even worth a detour for browsing and buying when you have the time.

Ice cream machines can be found at all the cooking-equipment places listed below. Also, you can do a Google search on ice cream machines and discover many sites where you can compare prices. I have found regular store prices are competitive with Internet shopping.

Agro World
19998 SOUTHWEST 256TH STREET
HOMESTEAD, FL 33031
www.agroworld.com
(305) 245-7746
Fresh and frozen tropical fruits, including passion fruit.

Bridge Kitchenware
214 EAST FIFTY-SECOND STREET
NEW YORK, NY 10022
www.bridgekitchenware.com
(212) 688-4220
Cooking equipment.

Bubble Tea Supply
1466 LILIHIA STREET
HONOLULU, HI 96817
www.bubbletea.com
(877) 869-2622
Black and multicolored tapioca pearls, wide straws, and information about bubble tea.

Chef's Catalogue
www.chefscatalogue.com
(800) 884-2433
Baking and cooking equipment.

Chocosphere
www.chocosphere.com
(877) 992-4626
Many brands (Callebaut, E. Guittard, El Rey, Scharffen Berger, and Vahlrona) of chocolate. You can also go to the specific web site of each chocolate company.

Davidson Eggs
2963 BERNICE ROAD
LANSING, MI 60438
www.davidsoneggs.com
(800) 410-7619
Pasteurized eggs in the shell.

Dean & Deluca
NEW YORK, CALIFORNIA, NORTH CAROLINA, MISSOURI, AND WASHINGTON, D.C.; CHECK WEB SITE OR CALL FOR LOCATIONS.
www.dean-deluca.com
(800) 221-7714
Cooking equipment and ingredients.

Eggology
www.eggology.com
(888) 669-6557
Pasteurized egg whites.

Ginger People

2700 GARDEN ROAD, SUITE G
MONTEREY, CA 93940

www.gingerpeople.com

(800) 551-5284

Candied ginger.

India Spice House

www.indiaspicehouse.com
Spices.

J. B. Prince

36 EAST THIRTY-FIRST STREET
NEW YORK, NY 10016

www.jbprince.com

(800) 473-0577

Baking and cooking equipment.

King Arthur Flour

ROUTE 5 SOUTH
NORWICH, VT 05055

www.kingarthurflour.com

(800) 807-6836

Baking ingredients and equipment,
Guittard sprinkles.

KitchenAid

www.kitchenaid.com

(800) 541-6390

Baking and cooking equipment.

MexGrocer

www.MexGrocer.com

(858) 459-3489

Dulce de leche, cajeta, Ibarra chocolate.

Nellie and Joe's

P.O. BOX 2368
KEY WEST, FL 33045

www.keylimejuice.com

(800) 546-3743

Key lime juice.

Nielsen-Massey Vanillas

www.NielsenMassey.com

(800) 525-7873

Vanilla beans, extracts, pastes,
and powders.

Penzeys Spices

www.penzeys.com

(800) 741-7787

Spices.

Perfect Purée

www.perfectpuree.com

(707) 261-5100

Fruit purées. Perfect Purée can also be
found at www.amazon.com.

Prairie Moon

www.prairiemoon.biz

(800) 331-0767

Siphon CO_2 chargers in brushed
aluminum or bright colors.

Sadaf Company

www.sadaf.com

(800) 852-4050

Rose water.

Sur La Table

STORES ACROSS THE UNITED STATES; CHECK
WEB SITE OR CALL FOR LOCATIONS.

www.surlatable.com

(800) 243-0852

Cooking equipment and ingredients.

TotallyNawlins

www.totallynawlins.com

(866) 467-3489

Medaglia D'Oro instant espresso.

U.S. Farmers' Markets

www.ams.usda.gov/farmersmarkets

Williams-Sonoma

STORES ACROSS THE UNITED STATES; CHECK
WEB SITE OR CALL FOR LOCATIONS.

www.williamssonoma.com

(877) 812-6235

Cooking equipment and ingredients.

Zabar's

2245 BROADWAY
NEW YORK, NY 10024

www.zabars.com

(800) 697-6301

Cooking equipment and ingredients.

acknowledgments

Special thanks to all those who participated in the writing of this book: recipe testers Angela Brassinga, Susan Berger, David Cleveland, Gina Burrell, Joanna Rees-Gallanter, Taylor Jean Gallanter, Suzie Hurd Greenup, Erin Loftus, Kathleen Mariano, Suzannah McFerrin, Katie Petcavich, Janet Rikala Dalton, Renée Toomire, and Allen Underhill. Bill LeBlond, for his calm guidance. Jane Dystel, for her encouragement. Adair Lara, for her verbal clarity. Amy Treadwell, for always finding the answers. Michael Weisberg, for his continual enthusiasm. Sheri Giblin and Dan Becker for the photographs. Shirley Corriher, for her technical expertise. The Baker family, for clearing the brambles between our houses and expediting ice cream dessert deliveries. Sur La Table, for the use of their ice cream machine. KitchenAid for making high-quality products. And last but not least, Zach, Micah, JJ, Stephanie, Lauren, Andrea, Leah, Adam, Ethan, Jay, and Allison, for always trying every dessert I put in front of them.

bibliography

Included here are books I used in the research of *A Passion for Ice Cream,* as well as interesting and noteworthy books on the subject of frozen desserts.

Bloom, Carole. *The International Dictionary of Desserts, Pastries and Confections.* New York: Hearst Books, 1995.

Chapon, Philippe. *Le Livre d'Or de la Glace.* France: Editions du Chêne, Hachette Livre, 1998.

Corriher, Shirley O. *Cookwise.* New York: William Morrow and Company, 1997.

Culinary Institute of America. *Baking and Pastry: Mastering the Art and Craft.* Hoboken, NJ: John Wiley & Sons, 2004.

Daley, Regan. *In the Sweet Kitchen: The Definitive Baker's Guide.* New York: Artisan, 2001.

Damerow, Gail. *Ice Cream! The Whole Scoop.* Macomb, IL: Glenbridge Publishing Ltd., 1991.

David, Elizabeth. *Harvest of the Cold Months: The Social History of Ice and Ices.* New York: Viking Penguin, 1995.

Farrow, Joanna, and Sara Lewis. *Ice Cream and Iced Desserts.* New York: Lorenz Books, Anness Publishing, 2000.

Funderburg, Anne Cooper. *Chocolate, Strawberry, and Vanilla: A History of American Ice Cream.* Bowling Green, OH: Bowling Green State University Popular Press, 1995.

Funderburg, Anne Cooper. *Sundae Best.* Bowling Green, OH: Bowling Green State University Popular Press, 2002.

Harris, Henry G., and Borella Harris. *Ices, Jellies and Creams.* London: Kegan Paul Ltd., 2002.

Herbst, Sharon. *Food Lover's Companion.* New York: Barron's Educational Series, 1990.

International Dairy Foods Association. *The Latest Scoop.* Washington, D.C. 2002.

Johns, Pamela Sheldon. *Gelato! Italian Ice Creams, Sorbetti & Granite.* Berkeley, CA: Ten Speed Press, 2000.

Kimball, Chris. *The Dessert Bible.* New York: Little, Brown and Company, 2000.

Lenôtre, Gaston. *Ice Creams and Candies.* New York: Barron's, 1979.

Liddell, Caroline, and Robin Weir. *Frozen Desserts: The Definitive Guide to Making Ice Creams, Ices, Sorbets, Gelati, and other Frozen Delights.* New York: St. Martin's Press, 1995.

Linton, Marilyn, and Tanya Linton. *125 Best Ice Cream Recipes.* Toronto, Canada: Robert Rose, 2003.

Marshall, A. B. *The Book of Ices.* London: A. H. Mayer, 1885. Reprint edition, *Ices, Plain and Fancy.* New York: The Metropolitan Museum of Art, 1976.

McGee, Harold. *The Curious Cook: More Kitchen Science and Lore.* Reprint, New York: John Wiley & Sons, 1992.

——*On Food and Cooking.* New York: John Wiley & Sons, reprint edition, 1997.

Rombauer, Irma S., Marion Rombauer-Becker, and Ethan Becker. *The All New, All Purpose Joy of Cooking.* New York: Scribner, 1997.

Stogo, Malcolm. *Ice Cream and Frozen Desserts: A Commercial Guide to Production and Marketing.* New York: John Wiley & Sons, 1998.

Turback, Michael. *A Month of Sundaes.* New York: Red Rock Press, 2002.

index

table of equivalents

The exact equivalents in the following tables have been rounded for convenience.

liquid/dry measures

U.S.	METRIC
¼ teaspoon	1.25 milliliters
½ teaspoon	2.5 milliliters
1 teaspoon	5 milliliters
1 tablespoon (3 teaspoons)	15 milliliters
1 fluid ounce (2 tablespoons)	30 milliliters
¼ cup	60 milliliters
⅓ cup	80 milliliters
½ cup	120 milliliters
1 cup	240 milliliters
1 pint (2 cups)	480 milliliters
1 quart (4 cups, 32 ounces)	960 milliliters
1 gallon (4 quarts)	3.84 liters
1 ounce (by weight)	28 grams
1 pound	454 grams
2.2 pounds	1 kilogram

length

U.S.	METRIC
⅛ inch	3 millimeters
¼ inch	6 millimeters
½ inch	12 millimeters
1 inch	2.5 centimeters

oven temperature

FAHRENHEIT	CELSIUS	GAS
250	120	½
275	140	1
300	150	2
325	160	3
350	180	4
375	190	5
400	200	6
425	220	7
450	230	8
475	240	9
500	260	10